THE LIE OF FEAR

THE LIE OF FEAR

E. I. Osborne, Jr.

Trilogy Christian Publishers

A Wholly Owned Subsidiary of Trinity Broadcasting Network

2442 Michelle Drive

Tustin, CA 92780

Copyright © 2024 by E. I. Osborn, Jr.

All Scripture quotations, unless otherwise noted, taken from *The Holy Bible*, King James Version. Cambridge Edition: 1769.

All rights reserved, including the right to reproduce this book or portions thereof in any form whatsoever.

For information, address Trilogy Christian Publishing

Rights Department, 2442 Michelle Drive, Tustin, CA 92780.

Trilogy Christian Publishing/ TBN and colophon are trademarks of Trinity Broadcasting Network.

For information about special discounts for bulk purchases, please contact Trilogy Christian Publishing.

Trilogy Disclaimer: The views and content expressed in this book are those of the author and may not necessarily reflect the views and doctrine of Trilogy Christian Publishing or the Trinity Broadcasting Network.

10 9 8 7 6 5 4 3 2 1

Library of Congress Cataloging-in-Publication Data is available.

B-ISBN#: 979-8-89333-648-1

E-ISBN#: 979-8-89333-649-8

TABLE OF CONTENTS

INTRODUCTION	7
THE ORIGIN OF FEAR	9
CHRISTIANS SHOULD NOT FEAR DEATH	19
THE DEFINITION OF FEAR	23
INSTINCT and FEAR	27
THE FEAR OF THE LORD	29
STOCKHOLM SYNDROME	31
RESPECTFUL REVERENCE	33
THE LIE OF FEAR	35
THE LIE	37
THE GIFTS AND THE FRUIT OF THE SPIRIT	47
FEAR ONLY WORKS IF YOU BELIEVE THE LIE	51
DO NOT ALLOW OR TOLERATE FEAR	59
DELIVERANCE FROM FEAR	63
The Stronghold of Fear	67
THE WAY OUT	77
FEAR OR FAITH	85
WORRY IS FEAR	93
THE FEAR OF THE UNKNOWN	101

FEAR COMETH BY HEARING	109
GOD AND THE DEVIL WANT AND NEED THE SAME THING	111
PERFECT LOVE CASTS OUT FEAR	113
NOTES	115
CONTACT INFORMATION	117

INTRODUCTION

Many people, Christians and non-Christians alike, struggle with fear. That's why I am so grateful and excited about this book.

The powerful revelations and insights from the Bible about fear that this book contains will equip Believers and non-Believers alike to be delivered from the bondage of fear once and for all.

After you read this book, you will never be affected by fear again in the ways that you once were.

ALL FEAR IS OF THE DEVIL!

If you have any fear in your life, make no mistake about it: It DID NOT come from God!

In John 8:32, Jesus said, *"and ye shall know the truth, and the truth shall make you free."*

It is only the truth that you know that makes you free, and I believe the truth in this book will not only make you free, but it will also keep you free from the spirit of fear for the rest of your life.

In Hosea 4:6, God said, *"My people are destroyed for the lack of knowledge."*

It is amazing to think that one small, simple piece of information could make such a huge difference in the quality of life and peace of mind that a person experiences each day.

If you or anyone you know struggles with fear of any kind, then this book is the answer that you and they have been praying for. Once you know the revelations that you are about to learn through this book, it will be impossible for fear to ever affect you the way it did in the past.

If you receive these revelations and follow the instructions in this book, then fear will never control, dominate, or influence your life again.

Fear is a spirit of deception that is manifested when a person believes a lie.

THE ORIGIN OF FEAR

Where did fear come from? Is it one of the Fruit of the Spirit like love, joy, and peace? No, fear is not a fruit of the Spirit, nor is it an emotion. Fear is a spirit, and it is of the devil.

2 Timothy 1:7 says, *"For God hath not given us the spirit of fear; but of power, and of love, and of a sound mind."*

The Bible says fear is a spirit. It calls it "a spirit of fear," and:

All fear is of the devil.

There is no such thing as good fears and bad fears. The idea of good and bad fears is the result of us not understanding the difference between the spirit of fear and the emotions of being afraid or frightened, and they are two completely different things altogether. Being afraid or frightened are feelings that come from your internal emotions. While fear, on the other hand is an external force that, if tolerated and allowed, could become internal.

Feeling afraid usually happens as a result of something you see, hear, taste, smell, or touch, but the spirit of fear can come upon a person for absolutely no reason whatsoever.

Fear did not come from God. Fear, like sickness, disease, poverty, and lack, came into the world through the sin of Adam. The Bible says God is Love, and there is no fear in love. So, when God, who is Love formed man in His image and likeness from the dust of the ground and created all we see, know, consider, and understand: He didn't have any fear to put into Man or His creation, because God is Love, and there is no fear in love.

1 John 4:8 and 16 say, *"God is love."*

1 John 4:18 says, *"There is no fear in love; but perfect love casteth out fear: because fear hath torment. He that feareth is not made perfect in love."*

Genesis 1:26 says, *"And God said, Let us make man in our image, after our likeness: and let them have dominion over the fish of the sea, and over the fowl of the air, and over the cattle, and over all the earth, and over every creeping thing that creepeth upon the earth."*

God made man in His image and likeness and gave him dominion over all of His creation. The word dominion means: *to have complete authority or rule over.* The one who has complete authority and rules does not have fear of the things they rule over. It is the thing under authority that fears and reverences the ruler.

Genesis 9:2 says, *"And the fear of you and the dread of you shall be upon every beast of the earth, and upon every fowl of the air, upon all that moveth upon the earth, and upon all the fishes of the sea; into your hand are they delivered."*

God delivered every creature into the hands of Noah and his sons to rule over them after the flood. The fear and dread of mankind was upon all creatures. This is how it was with Adam as well. Adam had dominion, and that dominion caused Adam to be feared by every beast of the earth, every foul of the air, by all that moved upon the earth, and by all the fishes of the sea. The word "fear" in Genesis 9:2 means "reverence." It was an instinct in animals, not the spirit of fear. Adam did not have any fear, because there was absolutely nothing for him to be afraid of. There was no death, no fear of death, and no spirit of fear in the Garden of Eden.

I heard a preacher that I greatly respect and admire teaching a message about fear. He said scientifically we have two fears that we are born with, the fear of falling, and the fear of loud noises.

Well, he is absolutely right. We are born with them, but they are not fears, they are internal emotions. Today, we are born in sin under the Adamic curse with those fears that come from the fear of death, but when Adam was created, he had no fear at all, because there was no death and absolutely nothing for him to fear or be afraid of. The fear of falling and the fear of loud noises are the product of the fear of death, just like all other fears. These fears are internal parts of our emotions. They are not the spirit of fear.

Fear came into the world through Adam's sin, along with sickness, disease, poverty, lack, death, and every other wicked thing that you can name or imagine.

Romans 5:12 says, *"Wherefore, as by one man sin entered into the world, and death by sin; and so death passed upon all men, for that all have sinned."*

Sin came into the world and death by sin. Before Adam sinned, there was no death or anything that would cause death. The possibility of dying created the fear of death, and that is what all fear and the emotions of being afraid and frightened are born out of.

Where there is no fear of death, the spirit of fear and all of its components have nothing to operate from.

"The fear of death" is the root of all fear. If there is no death, then there is no fear.

Hebrews 2:14-15 says, *"Forasmuch then as the children are partakers of flesh and blood, he also himself likewise took part of the same; that through death he might destroy him that had the power of death, that is, the devil; and deliver them who through fear of death were all their lifetime subject to bond-*

age."

People are not afraid of heights, spiders, or flying; they are afraid of dying. The fear of death is what makes us vulnerable to the spirit of fear. The spirit of fear can only function in the lives of people that have a fear of death.

People are able to bungee jump, sky dive, and cliff dive because they have no fear of death. All of these things are called death-defying for a reason.

When God *"formed man of the dust of the ground, and breathed into his nostrils the breath of life; and man became a living soul,"* he had immortality. There was no death or anything that would cause death. No sickness, no disease, no accidents, and no venomous snakes or wild animals that might eat you.

Because there was no death or anything that would cause death, there was also absolutely nothing to be afraid of. So, not only was there no fear in the beginning but the emotions of being afraid or frightened did not exist either. That was all a part of man becoming mortal and Adam realizing he was naked.

A lot of people are afraid of serpent-like creatures, such as snakes and lizards, but when the serpent showed up in the Garden of Eden, the Woman wasn't afraid and didn't display any signs of fear whatsoever, but rather, she held a conversation with it. She didn't run away from the serpent screaming for Adam to come and save her. The serpent came and asked the Woman questions, and she answered, because she had no fear.

Genesis 3:1-5 says, *"Now the serpent was more subtle than any beast of the field which the LORD God had made. And he said unto the woman, Yea, hath God said, Ye shall not eat of every tree of the garden? And the woman said unto the serpent, We may eat of the fruit of the trees of the garden: but of the fruit of the tree which is in the midst of the garden, God hath said, Ye shall not eat of it, neither shall ye touch it, lest ye die. And the serpent said unto the woman, Ye shall not surely die: for God doth know that in the day ye eat thereof, then your eyes shall be opened, and ye shall be as gods, knowing good and evil."*

The Woman reacted to the serpent in this way, because there was no fear in the world at that time. Her reaction was not because of the subtlety of the serpent. It was because she had no fear and wasn't afraid. The first evidence of fear is immediately after Adam eats of the fruit of the tree of the knowledge of good and evil.

Genesis 3:6-11 says, *"And when the woman saw that the tree was good for food, and that it was pleasant to the eyes, and a tree to be desired to make one wise, she took of the fruit thereof, and did eat, and gave also unto her husband with her; and he did eat. And the eyes of them both were opened, and they knew that they were naked; and they sewed fig leaves together, and made themselves aprons. And they heard the voice of the LORD God walking in the garden in the cool of the day: and Adam and his wife hid themselves from the presence of the LORD God amongst the trees of the garden. And the LORD God called unto Adam, and said unto him, Where art thou? And he said, I heard thy voice in the garden, and I was afraid, because I was naked; and I hid myself."*

Adam said, *"I was afraid, because I was naked."* This is the first time being afraid is mentioned in the Bible, and it is not "The Fear of the Lord." Their being afraid came as a result of their disobedience and the ensuing penalty of death that God said would happen if they ate of the tree of the knowledge of good and evil. Before Adam sinned, there was no death nor anything to be afraid of. This is the proof that fear and being afraid came into the world after Adam sinned.

Sin, Fear, and Death entered into the world through Adam's sin. Sin lead to death, and the possibility of dying produced the fear of death. *"The fear of death"* is the root of all fear. Again, if there is no death, then there is no fear. People are not actually afraid of heights, spiders, or flying; they are afraid of dying.

God does not want His children to fear anything or anyone, but He does want us to respectfully reverence Him and all those to whom it is due. Satan, on the other hand, would love for us to fear everything and everyone, because that fear enables him to manipulate, control, and destroy us.

I heard someone say, "A little fear is good." That perspective comes from not knowing that fear is a spirit. I compare that statement to someone saying something like, "A little demonic activity is good."

In Jeremiah 31:3, God says, *"The LORD hath appeared of old unto me, saying, Yea, I have loved thee with an everlasting love: therefore with lovingkindness have I drawn thee."*

God does not use the fear of judgment and hell to get us to obey Him and do His will. That would only create resentment. God is love. He uses love to draw us to Him, not fear. God wants us to love Him, and He knows you can't make someone love you through fear. God knows that anyone or anything that you fear, you will inevitably despise and resent.

Even when He speaks of death or hell as a consequence for sin, He does it in love, not to invoke fear. God is love, and His only motivation for everything He does is LOVE. The thought of Jesus suffering and paying the price for our sin should serve as a reminder of how much God loves us. Jesus bore all of the consequences and punishment of our sin so that we wouldn't have to.

1 John 4:19 says, *"We love him, because he first loved us."*

The first and great commandment in Mark 12:30 is, *"and thou shalt love the Lord thy God with all thy heart, and with all thy soul, and with all thy mind, and with all thy strength: this is the first commandment."*

I believe God loves us with all His heart, soul, mind and strength, so He is only commanding us to love Him in the same way that He loves us. He wants love to be our only motivation for the things we do for Him, not fear or reward. Jesus asked Simon Peter if He loved Him three times in John 21, beginning at verse fifteen.

John 21:15 says, *"So when they had dined, Jesus saith to Simon Peter, Simon, son of Jonas, lovest thou me more than these? He saith unto him, Yea, Lord; thou knowest that I love thee. He saith unto him, Feed my lambs."*

Jesus wants love to be Simon Peter's only reason for feeding His lambs, not guilt, condemnation, fear, or reward.

Fear cannot produce faith. The Bible says, *"fear hath torment."* The only thing that fear produces is torment. Fear is like faith's evil twin. It does the same thing as faith, but for the devil. Fear allows us to receive from the devil in the same way that faith allows us to receive from God.

Hebrews 11:6 says, *"But without faith it is impossible to please him: for he that cometh to God must believe that he is, and that he is a rewarder of them that diligently seek him."* In the same way that faith pleases God and allows Him to perform His will and plan in our lives, fear pleases the devil and allows him to perform his will and plan in our lives. Fear, is believing or having faith in Satan's ability to do his work and will in our lives. I have heard several people call fear, perverted faith. *Perverted Faith is fear that comes by hearing and believing a lie.*

Romans 10:17 says, *"So then faith cometh by hearing, and*

hearing by the word of God."

Perverted Faith also comes by hearing. The difference is, faith comes by hearing and believing the truth, and fear, or perverted faith, comes by hearing and believing a lie.

Romans 5:12 says, *"Wherefore, as by one man sin entered into the world, and death by sin; and so death passed upon all men, for that all have sinned."*

Sin and death entered into the world by the sin of one man, Adam. And so sin, death, and the fear of death passed upon all men, for all have sinned and are appointed to die.

Fear causes your body to produce adrenalin.

Adrenalin is: *a hormone secreted by the adrenal glands, especially in conditions of stress, increasing rates of blood circulation, breathing, and carbohydrate metabolism and preparing muscles for exertion.*

Fear is not the only thing that causes your body to produce adrenalin. The emotions of being afraid and frightened will also cause your body to produce adrenalin.

When God formed man and placed him in the Garden of Eden, there was no fear, stress, toil, or anything to be afraid of. Therefore, there was no need for adrenalin. The need for adrenalin came after Adam sinned and fell from grace. Fear, toil, and stress are all a part of the curse of sin.

I heard someone say, "God gave us fear to produce adrenalin, which we need in times of danger for fight or flight." The first problem with this idea is that God doesn't have fear to give. All fear, just like sickness, poverty, and lies are of the devil. The second thing is that there was no need for adrenalin until after the fall, because there was nothing in the Garden of Eden to fear or fight.

John 8:44 says, *"Ye are of your father the devil, and the lusts of your father ye will do. He was a murderer from the beginning, and abode not in the truth, because there is no truth in him. When he speaketh a lie, he speaketh of his own: for he is a liar, and the father of it."*

Jesus said the devil is the father of lies. The word father is translated from the Greek word **pater**. It means: *generator or male ancestor: the founder of a family or tribe, progenitor of a people: father parent: the originator or transmitter of anything.*

The devil is the father of lies, and he is also the father of fear.

He is the generator, founder, progenitor, father, parent, originator, and transmitter of all fear.

Fear and lies are siblings. They have the same father, which means they have the same DNA. That's why they work so well together and you will never see one without the other.

The definition of a lie is: *a situation involving deception.* A lie, which is deception, is the main component and root of all fear. We will talk more about that in a later chapter.

CHRISTIANS SHOULD NOT FEAR DEATH

There is absolutely no reason for a Christian to fear death. Lack of knowledge and unbelief are the two main reasons of Christians fearing death.

I believe dying and death are two different things. Dying is the process that leads to death. It can be slow or quick, painful or painless.

Death, on the other hand is completely different. According to the Bible there are three types of death, physical, spiritual, and the second death. Born Again Believers have no reason to fear death of any kind.

Physical death occurs when your body ceases to have the ability to sustain life. Spiritual death is when you are separated from God spiritually because of sin. The second death is when sinners are cast into the lake of fire for all eternity. When a Believer dies, they leave their physical body and go directly into the presence of the Lord.

2 Corinthians 5:8 says, *"we are confident, I say, and willing rather to be absent from the body, and to be present with the Lord."*

You are a spirit, you live in a natural body, and you have a soul. When your body no longer has the ability to sustain life, your spirit and soul depart. We call that physical death. At death, your spirit returns to God, and your eternal soul enters eternity where it goes into the presence of the Lord or to Hades to await resurrection and judgment.

If you are born again, you have no reason to fear death,

because death is only the transition from time to eternity in the presence of the Lord.

Daniel 12:2 says, *"And many of them that sleep in the dust of the earth shall awake, some to everlasting life, and some to shame and everlasting contempt."*

If you are not born again, then you should fear death, because death means your time to be forgiven of your sins is over, you have entered into eternity without your sins being forgiven, and you will spend eternity in everlasting contempt.

In Luke 16:22, when Lazarus the beggar died, he was carried by the angels into Abraham's Bosom or Paradise, which at that time was located in the lower parts of the earth. The rich man in Luke 16:23 also died, was buried, and went to hell, or Hades.

Today, because of Jesus, when a believer dies, they go immediately into the presence of God.

For the person that has been forgiven of their sins and accepted Jesus as Savior and Lord, death is merely the transition from time to eternity. It is going from being present in the body and absent from the Lord to being absent from the body and present with Lord. When you understand what death is, and you know that you're going to spend eternity with the Lord Jesus, that makes you free from the fear of death.

Revelations 21:8 says, *"But the fearful, and unbelieving, and the abominable, and murderers, and whoremongers, and sorcerers, and idolaters, and all liars, shall have their part in the lake which burneth with fire and brimstone: which is the second death."*

The "Second Death" is when the unrighteous are cast into the lake of fire for all eternity. Daniel 12:2 calls it *"shame and everlasting contempt."* It is when the unrighteous are separated from God for all eternity without any hope of reconciliation. With spiritual death, there is the opportunity for redemption and reconciliation, but not with the second death.

Hebrews 2:14-15 says, *"Forasmuch then as the children are partakers of flesh and blood, he also himself likewise took part of the same; that through death he might destroy him that had the power of death, that is, the devil; and deliver them who through fear of death were all their lifetime subject to bondage."*

The bondage of fear is living your life with the fear of death or dying. All fear comes from the fear of death. Anyone who has a fear of death is living in bondage. The bondage of fear will control your life and all of your choices and decisions every day.

Jesus took on flesh so that He could suffer and die in our place. Without putting on flesh, it would have been impossible for Him to die. It was through His death that He destroyed the devil that had the power and authority over death, so that we through His victory could be delivered from the bondage of the fear of death. Now, through Jesus, we have the promise of eternal life, and we know that death is merely the transitioning from time to eternity.

Revelations 1:18 says, *"I am he that liveth, and was dead; and,* behold, I am alive for evermore, Amen; and have the keys of hell and of death."

Jesus defeated death! He took the keys and authority over hell and death from the devil. Jesus has absolute authority over the devil, hell, and death for evermore.

The fear of death is broken!

THE DEFINITION OF FEAR

The dictionary definition of the word fear is: *a distressing emotion aroused by impending danger, evil, pain, etc., whether the threat is real or imagined; the feeling or condition of being afraid.*

Based on this dictionary definition, fear is a distressing emotion, or the feeling or condition of being afraid. The Bible, on the other hand says that fear is a spirit.

2 Timothy 1:7 says, *"For God hath not given us the spirit of fear; but of power, and of love, and of a sound mind."*

The dictionary says that fear is "a distressing emotion aroused by impending danger, evil, pain, etc., whether the threat is real or imagined." I believe the distressing emotion aroused by impending danger is just that, an emotion. Fear is a spirit. Fear can be felt when there is no impending danger, evil, pain, or threat of any kind. Fear attacks people and causes them to panic for absolutely no reason. If something you see, hear, taste, touch, or smell scares you, then that's being caused by your emotions. But if you don't see, hear, taste, touch, or smell something and you feel afraid, then that's a spirit of fear. There is a difference between the spirit of fear and your emotions, feelings, and physical condition. I believe fear is a spirit just as the Bible says.

In the dictionary, the definition says the cause of fear could be a real or imagined threat. So, the question is: What would cause an imagined threat?

Imagined is defined: (of something unreal or untrue) believed to exist or be so.

Well, based on the word imagined, I would have to say it is a thought or an idea that has somehow gotten into your mind. And because the threat is imagined and not real, then that would make it a lie.

The spirit of fear always has a lie attached to it in order for it to work.

The spirit of fear always comes with and through a lie. The lie might be that you're going to have an accident, the plane is going to crash, or some other type of tragedy is going to happen.

People who don't understand or believe in spiritual things might call feeling fearful and afraid for no reason an **instinct**.

An instinct is: *a natural or inherent aptitude, impulse, or capacity.*

The word fear in 2 Timothy 1:7 is translated from the Greek word *deilia,* and it is defined as timidity, fearfulness, and cowardice. These are all things that the spirit of fear produces. The spirit of fear causes a person to be timid, bashful, cowardly, and shy.

Emotions are affected by outward stimulation and operate from the inside out.

The spirit of fear comes upon you and affects you from the outside in. I have felt the spirit of fear trying to come upon me. It was only the grace of God and knowing the Truth that kept me free.

One day as I was driving, I felt the spirit of fear starting at the top of my head. It was like when the heat or air conditioning comes out of the vents in the ceiling. It slowly came down on to my head and continued to move down towards my shoulders. Just as it began to touch my shoulders, I opened my mouth, rebuked it in the Name of Jesus, and it left instantly. Emotions don't do that.

Emotions and feeling have to be triggered by something that you see, feel, taste, touch, or smell, but the spirit of fear is something that you can feel without your emotions and feelings being involved.

At least twice in my life I have felt fear for absolutely no reason. I didn't see anything, hear anything, touch anything, taste, or smell anything, and yet I felt fear.

Ever since then, I have been convinced that fear is a spirit just like the Bible says. Fear is not an emotion, feeling, or condition. *Fear is a spirit.*

The spirit of fear does not always come gradually; it can come in an instant as well. This usually happens when dealing with the unknown. When you are unfamiliar with your surroundings or uncertain as to what might happen in a situation, then all of a sudden, you're fearful.

When a person experiences fear for absolutely no reason, that might be labeled a panic attack. A panic attack is defined: *a sudden feeling of acute and disabling anxiety.* This happens without a cause and for no reason.

Another definition of a panic attack is: a sudden episode of intense fear or anxiety and physical symptoms, based on a perceived threat rather than imminent danger. So, there is no real threat or danger, just the perception.

If fear were just an emotion it would need something to trigger it. If you were to suddenly feel angry, cry, or even laugh for absolutely no reason, that might be considered a sign of an emotional problem. When a person feels fear for absolutely no reason, it is not because they have an emotional problem. It is because a spirit of fear has attacked them.

Fear, emotions, and instincts are three completely different things with completely different triggers.

INSTINCT AND FEAR

Some people might call fear an instinct or an instinctual reaction to the unknown. So let's consider what the definition of an instinct is.

The word **instinct** means: "an innate, typically fixed pattern of behavior in animals in response to certain stimuli: inborn complex patterns of behavior that exist in most members of a species, and should be distinguished from reflexes, which are simple responses of an organism to a specific stimulus: an inborn pattern of activity or tendency to action common to a given biological species: a natural or innate impulse, inclination, or tendency: a natural aptitude or gift" (languages.oup.com).

Based on these definitions of the word instinct, we can conclude that fear and instincts are two completely different things. Fear is a spirit, and instincts are fixed, complex patterns of behavior in response to certain stimuli, an inborn pattern of activity or tendency to action or a natural aptitude or gift. Instincts require some form of stimulus just like your emotions. Where, on the other hand, fear is a spirit and does not require any complex patterns of behavior, or inborn tendencies and actions.

The spirit of fear can strike at any time for absolutely no reason. It might be described as a sudden period of intense fear and discomfort that may include palpitations, sweating, chest pain or chest discomfort, shortness of breath, trembling, dizziness, numbness, confusion, or a feeling of impending doom or of losing control. The reason I believe this is caused by a spirit of fear is because it cannot be traced back to a particular source of any kind.

The word panic is defined as: "sudden overwhelming fear, with or without cause, that produces hysterical or irrational behavior." The key part of that definition is "with or without cause." Whenever someone panics and a natural cause for the panic cannot be determined, it is because the source or cause is spiritual. When an animal senses danger and reacts to it, we call that instinct, but if that same animal reacted in the same way for no reason; what would we call that? In the case of a person, we might call it anxiety or a panic attack, and yes, animals can have anxiety as well.

Either way, if there is no rational or natural source that is causing the fearful behavior, then the source must be spiritual.

THE FEAR OF THE LORD

In Proverbs 1:7, King Solomon wrote, *"The fear of the LORD is the beginning of knowledge."*

The word fear in this verse is translated from the Hebrew word *yirah*. It means to have respectful reverence. It does not mean to be afraid or frightened of God.

A great example of the fear of the Lord is the respectful reverence that you show a judge while in his courtroom. When you are in a courtroom and the bailiff says, "All rise," everyone stands to his or her feet in respectful reverence to the judge. We don't stand because we are afraid him. It is a sign of respect. We don't call the respectful reverence that we show towards a judge fear. The respectful reverence of the judge is exactly what the scripture is describing with the word fear. In the same way that we fear the judge, we fear the Lord, respectfully and reverentially.

God is love. He does not want us to fear Him; He wants us to love Him. I don't believe it is possible to actually love something or someone that you fear.

Even if you think you love someone that you fear, that fear will inevitably prevent you from trusting and developing a meaningful relationship with them. Fear is used to intimidate and control. The only thing that fear will produce is resentment.

In Jeremiah 31:3, the Word of God says, *"The LORD hath appeared of old unto me, saying, Yea, I have loved thee with an everlasting love: therefore with lovingkindness have I drawn thee."*

God does not use fear or the threat of punishment and hell to win us and draw us to Him. God draws us to Him with "lovingkindness" and wins us with His love.

If God tried to draw us through fear and intimidation, it would never work. Fear causes offense and resentment, not love.

1 John 4:18 says, *"There is no fear in love; but perfect love casteth out fear: because fear hath torment. He that feareth is not made perfect in love."*

First of all, this verse says, "there is no fear in love," and 1 John 4:8 and 16 say, **"God is Love."** So, if God is love and there is no fear in love, then it is impossible for fear to have come from God.

Secondly, if there is no fear in love, then anyone who believes they love something that they fear is deceived. Fear cannot produce love. So, whatever that feeling is, it can't be love.

What you might be feeling is some sort of perverted emotional and physical connection that you are mistakenly thinking is love. Psychologically, this might be referred to as Stockholm Syndrome.

STOCKHOLM SYNDROME

Stockholm Syndrome is a psychological response to being held captive. People with Stockholm Syndrome form a psychological connection with their captors and begin sympathizing with them. Stockholm Syndrome is not an official mental health diagnosis. Instead, it is thought to be a coping mechanism. Individuals who are the victims of fear or terror may develop it.

A person suffering from Stockholm Syndrome sympathizes with their captors and may actually believe that their captors care about them. It is similar to someone in an abusive relationship. Somehow, they have been deceived into believing that their abuser cares for them or even loves them. They may even believe that their abuser is abusing them because of how much they love them. Sadly, all of that is untrue.

RESPECTFUL REVERENCE

Respectful reverence is what we should have for anything that could harm us, not fear—things like electricity, lightning, firearms, or wild animals.

If you are an electrician, you don't fear electricity, but you do have a respectful reverence for it.

The lion tamer is able to get into the cage with the lions because he isn't afraid of them. But he does, however, have a respectful reverence for the lions.

Romans 13:7 says, *"Render therefore to all their dues: tribute to whom tribute is due; custom to whom custom; fear to whom fear; honour to whom honour."*

The word fear in this verse is translated from the Greek word *phobo*, which in some translations is translated as reverence. So God is not commanding us to fear anyone; He is commanding us to render respect and reverence to those to whom it is due.

THE LIE OF FEAR

Many people, Christians and non- Christians alike, struggle with fear. That is why I am so grateful and excited about this book.

This book contains wisdom, knowledge, and revelations from the Lord that will remove bondage, destroy yokes, and cast down every evil stronghold of fear. The Truth and simple revelations in this book are going to deliver and set people free from the spirit of fear once and for all.

In Hosea 4:6, God said, *"for my people are destroyed for the lack of knowledge."* It is amazing to think that one small, simple piece of information could make such a huge difference in the quality of life and peace of mind that people have.

If you or anyone you know struggles with fear of any kind, then this book contains the God-given answer that you and they have been praying for.

Once you know what you're about to learn through this book, it will be virtually impossible for fear to ever affect you again in the way it once did.

If you will receive the revelations in this book, then the spirit of fear will never dominate, control, or influence your life again as it did in the past.

THE LIE

All fear is based upon the fear of death and a lie that you have chosen to believe. So, if you have any fear in your life, it is because you have a fear of death and a lie that you have allowed yourself to believe.The reason completely healthy people with no life-threatening medical problems have a fear of dying young is because they fear death, and they believe the lie that they will die while they are young. There are also people who, for no reason at all, always have a fear that something bad is going to happen to them. That too is the result of the fear of death and a lie.

Having a fear of dying young and always fearing that something bad is going to happen come as the result of believing a lie. The root cause for the fear of doom and the fear of death is a lie and the lack of knowledge. Helping people to overcome their lack of knowledge is the main reason why God commissioned me to write this book and entitle it "The Lie of Fear."

The purpose of this book is to reveal the truth about fear and expose the lie that allows fear to exist and torment people.

I was watching television one night and came across a preacher teaching a message on fear. This program was not one that I normally watch, and the preacher was not someone that I follow, but I felt impressed to watch.

As I watched, the preacher told a story about being attacked by fear while he was on vacation with his wife. He said the thing that caused the fear was a thought.

The preacher told how he and his wife were swimming back to their boat when, all of a sudden, he had a thought that there were sharks in the water. He never saw any sharks or even dorsal fins. It was just the thought that there were sharks in the water that caused him to fear. As a result of the fear, he said he took off swimming so fast that he left his wife behind, struggling to get to the boat by herself.

When he got to the boat and realized he was alone, his wife yelled, "Hey, you left me." So he jumped back into the water and swam back to help her.

The preacher was swimming with his wife, who was struggling in the water, when all of a sudden, the thought of sharks caused him to take off and leave her behind.

As it turns out, there were no sharks in the water, and he was later told that there was no possibility of sharks being in that water. It was merely the lying thought of sharks that caused him to panic, experience fear, and abandon his wife.

The thought of sharks being in the water was a lie, but because he believed it, he felt fear.

That is how the lie of fear works. Some people would call that False Evidence Appearing Real, which I've heard used as an acronym for the word fear. But in this case, there was no false evidence appearing real, just a thought that turned out to be a lie.

The story told by this pastor on television was a confirmation to me about the message and purpose of this book.

His story confirms and reveals exactly how the lie of fear works.

When I think back and remember all of the people that I have ministered to over the years who were struggling with fear, I realize that all of their fears were based on a lie, just like this pastor.

The purpose of fear is to gain control through intimidation, domination, manipulation, and torment.

1 Kings 19:1-3 says, *"And Ahab told Jezebel all that Elijah had done, and withal how he had slain all the prophets with the sword. Then Jezebel sent a messenger unto Elijah, saying, So let the gods do to me, and more also, if I make not thy life as the life of one of them by to morrow about this time. And when he saw that, he arose, and went for his life, and came to Beer-sheba, which belongeth to Judah, and left his servant there."*

When Elijah heard Jezebel's threat to take his life, the Bible says, "he arose, and went for his life." The reason Elijah ran for his life was fear. The threat itself didn't create fear; it was his believing the threat that produced fear. Elijah should have realized that Jezebel's threat was a lie because God would protect him, but instead, he believed it.

Fear always has a lie connected to it. Anxiety, worry, terror, and intimidation all have lies connected to them. Each one produces a manifestation of the spirit of fear.

People struggle with many different types of fears. Some of the most common fears are: Aerophobia (fear of flying), Acrophobia (fear of heights), Achluophobia (fear of the dark), and Arachnophobia (fear of spiders). All of these fears are manifestations of the spirit of fear. They are all born out of a lie and the fear of death.

All of these phobias are able to effectively torment people through a lie that they believe. The lie might be the plane is going to crash, there's a monster in the dark room, or they're going to fall from that height and die. Whatever fear it happens to be, there is always a lie associated with it.

All fear is conceived from a lie that a person has been deceived into believing. The lie is always about something that will cause death. If you have any fear in your life, the basis of that fear comes from a lie that you have allowed yourself to believe and the fear of death.

Some people were afraid of the dark when they were children. Some had a fear of the so-called boogieman or of a monster being in the closet or under the bed. Many people carry these childhood fears into adulthood because they never stopped believing the lie that produced that fear.

Make no mistake about it: All of these fears are the product of a lie that they continue to believe as adults.

When I was in my early teens, I remember my father telling me about something he did not like and the reason he didn't like it. Basically, I believe he didn't like it because it was something that caused him to fear.

Unfortunately, after he told me about it, I found myself dealing with that fear as well. My father's fear was passed on to me by his simply telling me about it. Today, by the grace of God, I no longer have that fear.

My father had a feeling; that feeling created a thought; and that thought produced fear. Even before I experienced that feeling, I developed a fear about it. The fear I experienced was based solely on a thought that was a lie. Without me having any actual physical experience, the thought produced fear in me as well. The whole thing was based on a lie.

As simple as it may sound, the answer to being delivered from a spirit of fear is to *stop believing the lie*. There are many things that can cause death. Believing the lie that one of those things will lead to your death is what produces fear.

For some people the difficulty in overcoming the lie is that the lie has become a stronghold.

That means the lie is no longer just a thought that a person can easily stop thinking and believing. Strongholds are thoughts, imaginations, and knowledge that have been fortified in order to protect them. In the Bible, any thought, imagination, or knowledge that is contrary to the Word of God and has been fortified in order to protect it is called a stronghold.

2 Corinthians 10:3-5 says, *"For though we walk in the flesh, we do not war after the flesh: (for the weapons of our warfare are not carnal, but mighty through God to the pulling down of strong holds;) casting down imaginations, and every high thing that exalteth itself against the knowledge of God, and bringing into captivity every thought to the obedience of Christ."*

A stronghold is a thought, imagination, or knowledge that a person believes so much that they build walls or a fort around to guard and protect it from being changed. The walls are made up of other thoughts and arguments that reinforce and defend the validity of whatever is believed.

A stronghold is defined as: *a place that has been fortified so as to protect it against attack: a place where a particular cause or belief is strongly defended or upheld*

Unfortunately, in many cases, that's what the lie of fear becomes: a stronghold. And once it becomes a stronghold, it takes the mighty weapons of our warfare, which are supernatural power and delegated authority, to bring deliverance.

2 Timothy 1:7 says, *"For God hath not given us the spirit of fear; but of power, and of love, and of a sound mind."* God DID NOT give us fear, because God had no fear to give. God gave us power, love, and self-control.

Fear is a spirit. Fear and the emotion of being afraid, frightened or scared are two different things. Psalm 91:5-6 says, *"Thou shalt not be afraid for the terror by night; Nor for the arrow that flieth by day; Nor for the pestilence that walketh in darkness; Nor for the destruction that wasteth at noonday."* You are not supposed to be afraid of anything or anyone. One of the reasons that you are not supposed to be afraid is because the greater One lives on the inside of you. 1 John 4:4 says, *"Ye are of God, little children, and have overcome them: because greater is he that is in you, than he that is in the world."*

You are of God and will overcome anything that may come against you, because the Greater One is on the inside of you! Jesus is not only the Greater One; He is the Greatest One!

Romans 10:17 says, *"So then faith cometh by hearing, and hearing by the word of God."*

Fear comes by hearing, just like faith.

Mark 9:23 says, *"Jesus said unto him, If thou canst believe, all things are possible to him that believeth."* **Your believing makes ALL THINGS possible. So stop believing the lie that is producing fear and start believing the Truth (God's Word). If you believe the devil can give you cancer or cause you to have an accident, then your believing makes it possible. Or, if you believe that Jehovah Rapha is the Lord that healeth thee and no weapon formed against thee shall prosper, then your believing makes that possible. God has set before us life and death, and He says to us: Choose life and live.**

Why believe that you're going to die when you can believe Psalm 118:17 that says, *"I shall not die, but live, And declare the works of the LORD."*

Why believe you're having a bad day when you can and should be believing Psalm 118:24 that says, *"This is the day which the LORD hath made; We will rejoice and be glad in it."*

It is your believing that makes things possible and creates your reality.

God and Satan want and need the same thing. They want and need you to believe what they say. It is your believing that allows them to do their will and carry out their plan in your life. We will say more about this in the next chapter.

1 John 4:18 says, *"There is no fear in love; but perfect love casteth out fear: because fear hath torment. He that feareth is not made perfect in love."*

God is LOVE, and there is no fear in love—God. Fear has torment, and the tormenter is the devil.

The mission of the spirit of fear is to get you to authorize the devil to do whatever he has told you or is showing you.

You grant him authorization through your words and or your actions. The devil needs you to believe his word just like God needs you to believe His Word. Satan is the thief who comes to steal, kill, and destroy.

In John 10:10 Jesus said, *"The thief cometh not, but for to steal, and to kill, and to destroy."*

Your believing authorizes Satan to do that in your life.

Satan is also the devourer in 1 Peter 5:8. *"Be sober, be vigilant; because your adversary the devil, as a roaring lion, walketh about, seeking whom he may devour."*

Job 3:25 says, *"For the thing which I greatly feared is come upon me, And that which I was afraid of is come unto me."*

Fear authorized the thing that Job greatly feared to come upon him and unto him.

Revelations 21:8 says, *"But the fearful, and unbelieving, and the abominable, and murderers, and whoremongers, and sorcerers, and idolaters, and all liars, shall have their part in the lake which burneth with fire and brimstone: which is the second death."*

The fearful are those who allowed fear to keep them from obeying God. Not obeying God is sin, and that's why they were cast into the lake which burneth with fire and brimstone. Revelations 21:8 says, *"the fearful, and unbelieving."* Fear and unbelief always go hand-in-hand.

Daniel 11:32 says, *"but the people that do know their God shall be strong, and do exploits."*

I wish it said "know and believe," because a lot of people know God, but they don't believe Him. It is knowing and believing God that makes you strong and capable of doing exploits.

Just as faith without works is dead, so also fear without works is dead. Fear like faith only works if it is accompanied by works or corresponding action. Fear wants you to act based on the lie that you believe and not on the Truth, God's Word.

When you really believe the lie of fear, it will produce some type of corresponding action. Just like when you believe the Word of God.

2 Timothy 1:7 says, *"For God hath not given us the spirit of fear; but of power, and of love, and of a sound mind."*

The biggest lie or misconception that causes people to accept and tolerate the spirit of fear is that *fear came from God.*

We have been told things like, fear is a God-given emotion or that having a little fear can be a good thing. These ideas are completely untrue, and in some ways may even be dangerous.

It was and still is impossible for God to give us fear, because He has no fear to give. 2 Timothy 1:7 confirms and establishes this point. It clearly states, *"For God hath not given us the spirit of fear."*

All fear is of the devil. It came into the world through the sin of Adam along with death, sickness, disease, poverty, and all evil.

(Read chapter 3, The Origin of Fear)

Romans 5:12 says, *"Wherefore, as by one man sin entered into the world, and death by sin; and so death passed upon all men, for that all have sinned."*

By one man, sin entered into the world, and death by sin; and so death and the fear of death passed upon all men.

The fear of death is the root of all fear. So, if you overcome the fear of death, you take away the spirit of fear's ability to function in your life. The fear of flying, the fear of thunder and lightning, and the fear of spiders are all products of the fear of death. People that fear spiders believe that the spider can do something that will lead to their death.

If there were no death, would anyone be afraid of flying? No!

Consider all the things that you fear and then ask yourself this question: If I didn't fear death, would any of these things still scare me? The answer is no. And yes, I realize that you still may not like spiders or rodents, but it is the fear of death that makes you run from a spider, while someone that doesn't fear death runs after it and kills it.

The only difference between the two people is the lie that one of them believes.

Teaching people the laws of aerodynamics and the scientific causes of thunder and lightning can also help them to overcome those fears. This helps because having an understanding of how something works eliminates the threat of death that exists due to a lack of knowledge.

The spirit of fear comes and stays upon you as long as you continue to believe the lie. If you were to show me someone that is struggling with fear, I guarantee you there is a lie that they are believing. That lie is the source and cause of their fear.

THE GIFTS AND THE FRUIT OF THE SPIRIT

2 Timothy 1:7 says, *"For God hath not given us the spirit of fear; but of power, and of love, and of a sound mind."*

Some translations of this verse use the words timidity and cowardice in place of or along with the word fear. Whichever translation you use, timidity and cowardice are fear.

Fear is not a feeling or an emotion. Fear is a spirit, and fear is also faith's counterpart. Just as the Holy Spirit has fruit and gifts, the devil (who is a spirit), has fruit and gifts, fear being the counterpart to the gift and fruit of faith. So the word fear could represent the spirit of fear, or it could represent faith's counterpart depending on the context.

2 Corinthians 4:13 says, *"We having the same spirit of faith, according as it is written, I believed, and therefore have I spoken; we also believe, and therefore speak."*

The spirit of faith in this verse is referring to a manifestation of the gift or fruit of faith.

Faith is one of the gifts and fruit of the Holy Spirit. Fear is the spirit of faith's counterpart. So when I say fear is faith's twin, I am referring to fear as a gift or fruit of the spirit of fear.

1 Corinthians 12:7-9 says, *"But the manifestation of the Spirit is given to every man to profit withal. For to one is given by the Spirit the word of wisdom; to another the word of knowledge by the same Spirit; to another faith by the same Spirit; to another the gifts of healing by the same Spirit."*

Galatians 5:22-23 says, *"But the fruit of the Spirit is love, joy, peace, longsuffering, gentleness, goodness, faith, meekness, temperance: against such there is no law."*

Hebrews 11:1 says, *"Now faith is the substance of things hoped for, the evidence of things not seen."*

I could use this same verse to describe the gift of fear as well, because fear is faith's counterpart. Now *fear* is the substance of things hoped for, the evidence of things not seen.

Some of the other fruit and gifts of the spirit of fear are: suicide, anxiety, worry, low self-esteem, shyness, timidity, impatience, depression, hate, turmoil, wickedness, evil, pride, jealousy, envy, lying, insanity, murder, confusion, obsession, narcissism, lust, racism, sexual immorality, and divination, just to name a few.

1 Corinthians 12:4-6 says, *"Now there are diversities of gifts, but the same Spirit. And there are differences of administrations, but the same Lord. And there are diversities of operations, but it is the same God which worketh all in all."*

This is true for the gifts and fruit of the spirit of fear as well. There are diversity of gifts, administrations, and operations but also the same spirit of fear and the same devil, which worketh all in all.

God is a Spirit, and Satan is a spirit. Satan wants to be God, so he imitates everything that God does. In the Kingdom of God, there is the Father, the Son, and the Holy Spirit. In Satan's kingdom, he would be the equivalent to the Father, the antichrist would be the son, and I believe the spirit of fear would be the equivalent to the Holy Spirit. The Holy Spirit makes you bold and courageous, the spirit of fear makes you timid, shy, and cowardly.

Just like faith is a gift of the Holy Spirit, fear is a gift of the spirit of fear. Faith is also a fruit of the Holy Spirit, and fear is a fruit of the spirit of fear. Gifts and fruit are manifestations of the spirit, whether of the Holy Spirit or the spirit of fear.

Fear is Faith's evil twin.

FEAR ONLY WORKS IF YOU BELIEVE THE LIE

Fear, like faith, only works if you believe. Just like faith without works is dead, so too fear without works is dead, being alone.

James 2:17 says, *"Even so faith, if it hath not works, is dead, being alone."*

IN ORDER FOR FAITH TO WORK, YOU HAVE TO BELIEVE, AND IN ORDER FOR FEAR TO WORK, YOU HAVE TO BELIEVE.

What do you have to believe in order for faith to work, and what do you have to believe for fear to work? Faith works when you believe God's Word, and fear works when you believe the devil's lie that is always contrary to the Word of God.

Psalm 91:5-6 says, *"Thou shalt not be afraid for the terror by night; Nor for the arrow that flieth by day; Nor for the pestilence that walketh in darkness; Nor for the destruction that wasteth at noonday."*

God says, *"Thou shalt not be afraid."* You are not supposed to be afraid of anything or anyone. God is constantly reminding us in His Word not to fear.

I have heard people say there are three hundred and-sixty-five verses in the Bible where it says fear not or a variation of fear not. That equals one fear not for each day of the year.

There are many reasons why you shouldn't fear. One of

them is because God said, "I will never leave thee, nor forsake thee." God said, "I Am with you always." As a matter of fact, God is not just with you; He is in you. The Greater One lives on the inside of you.

1 John 4:4 says, *"Ye are of God, little children, and have overcome them: because greater is he that is in you, than he that is in the world."*

You are of God little children, and you will overcome anything or anyone that comes against you, because the Greater One is on the inside of you! In fact, He's not just greater; He is the GREATEST. There is nothing and no one greater than our God. Stop believing the lie that you're not enough and you don't have what it takes. Christ in you makes you more than enough and gives you more than you need.

Mark 9:23 says, *"Jesus said unto him, If thou canst believe, all things are possible to him that believeth."*

When Jesus said *all things* are possible, that is exactly what He meant. Your believing makes all things possible. Whether it is good or bad, positive or negative, true or false. Your believing makes it possible. The impossible becomes possible when you believe, even if it is a lie.

Your believing a thing authorizes it, empowers it, allows it, and causes it to happen. Your believing, just like faith, is the substance of things hoped for. Faith or faith's counterpart fear make ALL things possible.

Fear works just like faith. Again, Hebrews 11:1 says, *"Now faith is the substance of things hoped for, the evidence of things not seen."*

Fear, like faith, is the substance of things hoped for, the evidence of things not seen. Just as God was able to accomplish all of the impossible things in Hebrews 11 through faith, Satan is able to accomplish his works through fear.

Hebrews 11:1 from an old Living Translation says, *"What is faith? It is the confident assurance that something we want is going to happen. It is the certainty that what we hope for is waiting for us, even though we cannot see it up ahead."*

Your fear, just like your faith, is the confident assurance that something you fear is going to happen. It is the certainty that what we fear is waiting for us, even though we cannot see it up ahead. And that is exactly why it happens.

Fear is the mirror image of faith.

The difference between faith and fear is: Faith believes God and His Word, and fear believes the devil and his lie.

We don't specifically say that we have faith in a lie coming to pass. We say things like, I'm afraid it's going to happen, or I fear that it will come to pass.

God needs us to have faith in order for Him to accomplish His Will in our life. Satan needs us to have fear in order for him to accomplish his will in our life. So, fear and faith have the same function. Faith and fear are the vehicles through which God and Satan accomplish their will and manifest their works in our lives. God uses faith, Satan uses fear. Satan needs fear for the same reason that God needs faith. That reason is, because we have freewill, and neither God nor the devil can violate our freewill.

Fear is Faith's evil twin! It is faith's reflection, faith's shadow. And just as faith comes by hearing, so does fear.

Romans 10:17 says, *"So then faith cometh by hearing, and hearing by the word of God."*

I could also say: so then fear cometh by hearing, and hearing by the lying word of the devil. Hearing is one of your five senses, and it is through your five senses that you receive the things that influence what you believe. What you see, hear, smell, taste, and touch determine what you believe. *It is when you act on those beliefs that it becomes faith.* In the book of John, it says many believed in his name when they saw the miracles that he did.

John 2:23 says, *"Now when he was in Jerusalem at the Passover, in the feast day, many believed in his name, when they saw the miracles which he did."*

The five senses are the gates to your soul. Your soul is your mind, your will, and your emotions. That's why in the book of Proverbs we are told to keep or guard our hearts, which refers to our souls. Something you hear, see, feel, taste, or touch can produce faith or fear.

Proverbs 4:23 says, *"Keep thy heart with all diligence; For out of it are the issues of life."*

2 Corinthians 5:7 says, *"for we walk by faith, not by sight."*

In order for faith to work, you have to walk by faith and not by sight.

Walking by faith and not by sight is believing and acting on the Truth with no visible or physical evidence of its reality. In order for fear to work you have to walk by fear and not by sight, which is the same thing as walking by faith, except your believing and acting is based on a lie.

Just as faith without works is dead, fear without works is dead. Another translation used for works is, corresponding action.

When you really believe the Word of God, you will act on it, and when you really believe the lying word of the devil, you will act on it as well. Believing combined with corresponding action is faith or fear. Believing the truth produces faith and believing a lie produces fear.

Mark 11:23 says, *"For verily I say unto you, That whosoever shall <u>say</u> unto this mountain, Be thou removed, and be thou cast into the sea; and shall not doubt in his heart, but shall believe that those things which he <u>saith</u> shall come to pass; he shall have whatsoever he <u>saith</u>."*

The same principles and laws that work with faith also work with fear. So if you speak in faith or in fear and don't doubt, you will have what you say.

Faith filled words will make things happen, and fear filled words will do the same.

Proverbs 18:21 says, *"Death and life are in the power of the tongue: And they that love it shall eat the fruit thereof."*

The power is in the tongue and in believing that what you say will happen. Faith filled words produce life and fear filled words produce death. The tongue has the power to produce whatever you speak in faith or in fear.

Words are seeds, and your tongue is the instrument through which those seeds are sown.

One day the Lord said to me: *"Don't ever say anything that you don't want to happen."*

Hebrews 11:3, *"Through faith we understand that the worlds were framed by the word of God, so that things which are seen were not made of things which do appear."*

Just like God, you frame your world through words of faith or words of fear. So things that you see were not made of things which do appear.

In Mark 11:24, Jesus said, *"Therefore I say unto you, What things soever ye desire, when ye pray, believe that ye receive them, and ye shall have them."*

Praying is saying. So when you say and believe that you receive the things that you say, you will have them.

John 8:44 says, *"Ye are of your father the devil, and the lusts of your father ye will do. He was a murderer from the beginning, and abode not in the truth, because there is no truth in him. When he speaketh a lie, he speaketh of his own: for he is a liar, and the father of it."*

Not only is the devil a liar but he is also the Father of Lies. Jesus said, "there is no truth in him." That means everything the devil speaks is a lie. Lies are the seeds that produce fear. Lies and fear always go hand-in-hand, and the devil is the father of both of them.

Fear cannot exist without a lie. Fear needs a lie just like a flashlight needs batteries, an engine needs gas, and Rice Krispies need milk. Without the milk there's no snap, crackle, pop.

If I can convince a person that is bound by fear to stop believing the lie that is producing that fear, then that person will be set free. Fear cannot exist without a lie.

Even in a case where fear is being manifested through a feeling, that feeling is producing lying thoughts of impending hurt, harm, and death.

The feeling creates a thought, the thought is a lie, and believing the lie produces fear.

The dictionary definition of a lie is: *an intentionally false statement: present a false impression; be deceptive.*

The word "lie" in John 8:44 is translated from the Greek word *pseudos*. The Strong's Concordance defines it as: *con-*

scious and intentional falsehood: whatever is not what it seems to be.

In John 8:44, Jesus not only called the devil a liar; he called him the father of lies. Lies and fear have the same father, the devil.

"Ye are of your father the devil, and the lusts of your father ye will do. He was a murderer from the beginning, and abode not in the truth, because there is no truth in him. When he speaketh a lie, he speaketh of his own: for he is a liar, and the father of it."

Lying and fear are Satan's counterparts to God's Truth and faith. Everything that Satan does is based on a lie, just like everything that God does is based on His Word.

Fear is a spirit. Being afraid, frightened, and scared are emotions. The spirit of fear can come when there is absolutely nothing to be fearful or afraid of. Fear lies to you and makes you feel as though something bad is going to happen and you're going to get hurt or die. If you believe it, then fear is able to take hold. The goal of fear is to dominate and control your life so that Satan can steal, kill, and destroy you.

DO NOT ALLOW OR TOLERATE FEAR

Do not allow or tolerate fear in any area of your life.

Ephesians 4:27 says, *"neither give place to the devil."*

All fear is of the devil, so if you have fear in any area of your life, then you're giving place to the devil.

If you allow the devil to have place in your life, he will most certainly use that place to destroy you. That's why many people with fear eventually end up home-bound, room-bound, bed-bound, or dead if they are not delivered.

God does not use fear to motivate us to do His Will. God motivates us through love.

I John 4:18 says, *"There is no fear in love; but perfect love casteth out fear: because fear hath torment. He that feareth is not made perfect in love."*

This verse says, "There is **no fear** in love," and 1 John 4:8 and 16 say, **"God is love."** So, if there is no fear in love, then there is no fear in God. It also says, *"perfect love casteth out fear."* The reason it uses the term "casteth out" is because fear is a spirit, and it must be cast out.

2 Timothy 1:7 says, *"For God hath not given us the spirit of fear; but of power, and of love, and of a sound mind."*

Paul calls fear a spirit, and because fear is a spirit, it has to be cast out. Emotions and feelings can change, but fear has to be cast out.

God is love! So, if there is no fear in love, then there is no fear in God.

Hebrews 2:15 says, *"And deliver them who through fear of death were all their lifetime subject to bondage."*

All fear comes out of the fear of death! The fear of death produces bondage.

The fear of death exists because of the lack of knowledge or the rejecting of knowledge about death.

Every fear that a person has is because of a lie that they believe. The reason some people are afraid of the dark but not afraid of heights is because they believe a lie about the dark, but they don't believe a lie about heights.

If you hear a loud noise that startles you, that noise may cause you to be frightened and feel afraid. You can't stop that feeling from happening; it's just a natural reaction, but you can control how long the feeling lasts and how it affects you. Becoming afraid or frightened for a moment is natural, but you should not stay that way. Being afraid and frightened are emotional responses to the unknown. Not knowing what caused the loud noise can make you feel afraid or frightened momentarily, but once the source of the noise is known, then those feelings should leave. If you still feel afraid even after the source of the noise is known, then you're no longer dealing with emotions, you are dealing with a spirit of fear. Something can start out as an emotional reaction and then turn into a spiritual attack.

Emotions are triggered by something that you experience with your five senses. Fear, on the other hand, comes with no reason or explanation at all. Fear is a spirit.

Fear is a spirit. Fear and the emotions of being afraid, frightened, or scared are two different things.

Momentary feelings of being frightened or afraid can happen, but ongoing, long-term feelings of fear are an indication that a spirit of fear has crept in and is attempting to take up residence.

The danger in tolerating the emotions of being afraid and frightened is that, the longer you tolerate them, the more likely they are to become a stronghold, which could potentially make it a lot more difficult to overcome them.

Never allow or tolerate the feelings of being afraid, frightened, anxious, or worried to linger in your soul. Instead, pray, get knowledge, get wisdom, get understanding, and then use those things to get free. Always be proactive about overcoming negative emotions.

DELIVERANCE FROM FEAR

Now that we have talked about the origin of fear, the definition of fear, the fear of death, the fear of the Lord, and the lie of fear, let's turn our attention to being delivered from fear.

Deliverance from the spirit of fear is not as difficult as you may think. Deliverance starts with knowing and believing the Truth. Knowing the Truth is good, but it is your believing the Truth that really matters and actually makes the difference. Knowing and believing the Truth will make you free.

In John 8:32, Jesus said, *"and ye shall know the truth, and the truth shall make you free."*

Knowing and believing the Truth is the first step to everything in the Kingdom of God. Knowing and believing the Truth not only makes you free, but it keeps you free as well. Knowing and believing the Truth puts you in position to receive all that God has and all that God is. A lot of people know the Truth, but they don't believe it, and it is their unbelief that keeps them from salvation, healing, prosperity, and all of the manifold blessings of God.

The next step in being delivered from the spirit of fear is to stop believing the lie.

Some people know the Truth and believe it and yet somehow believe the devil's lie as well. They know the Truth but still accept the lie. The reason that happens is because the Truth is received by faith and the lie is received by facts. They are like the father in Mark 9:24 who said, *"Lord, I believe; help thou mine unbelief."* He believed Jesus was the Messiah, but also had unbelief as to whether or not Jesus could heal his son.

There are people that know the Truth but have more faith in the lie. I believe those people are walking more by sight than they are walking by faith.

2 Corinthians 5:7 says, *"for we walk by faith, not by sight."*

Sight is the sounds, feelings, and pains, etc. that are happening all around us, while the Truth is the covenants and promises that God has given to us in His Word. Even if the facts are diagnoses with all the x-rays, MRI's, and tests to prove it, the Truth is still: With the stripes of Jesus, you are healed.

When Fear comes based on facts or something that is true, it can easily be overcome by believing, confessing, and standing on the Word of God, which is Truth. Walking by faith is living your life in complete agreement and harmony with the Word of God. Walking by sight is living your life in complete agreement and harmony with everything you see, hear, taste, touch, or smell.

Truth cannot be overturned, because it is impossible for Truth to change. Something that is true can be true one moment and not true the next. Truth cannot change, ever. That's what makes it Truth.

The only Truth that exists in this world is the Word of God. The Word of God is immutable, infallible, and eternal. It is the same yesterday, and today, and forever. True is mutable, fallible, and temporary.

Walking by fear is the totally opposite of walking by faith. Fear has everything to do with your sight, senses, and emotions, while faith operates in the unseen, unknown realm.

The lie that creates fear is based on something you see, hear, touch, taste, or smell. The Truth, on the other hand, has nothing to do with your five senses, emotions, or feelings. The Truth has to be believed and received without any physical evidence. Truth is received by faith and faith alone. *Faith is knowing without seeing.* Faith believes and knows without any physical evidence or proof.

Hebrews 11:1 says, *"Now faith is the substance of things hoped for, the evidence of things not seen."*

THE STRONGHOLD OF FEAR

If the lie of fear has become a stronghold, the anointed Word of God will pull down the stronghold and set the captive free. The anointed Word of God destroys yokes and pulls down exaggerated imaginations, knowledge, and every lying thought that is contrary to the Word of God.

The Good News is: Fear and all the works of the devil have already been defeated. Your deliverance from fear was purchased for you almost two thousand years ago.

So, believe the Word of God, receive it, confess it, and stop believing the lie.

In the non-Christian, non-Bible-believing world, they advise people to face or confront their fears. This is known to have some success, because when you confront your fear, you find out that the thing that has been causing you to fear is a lie.

Believing that the impossible is possible can produce faith or fear. So, the devil uses fear just like God uses faith. Faith is always based on the Truth, and fear is always based on a lie. Deliverance from fear comes when the lie is exposed and the Truth is revealed and believed. There are also people who know and believe the Truth and yet still continue to believe the lie that opened the door and gave place to the spirit of fear.

James 1:6-8 says, *"But let him ask in faith, nothing wavering. For he that wavereth is like a wave of the sea driven with the wind and tossed. For let not that man think that he shall receive any thing of the Lord. A double minded man is unstable in all his ways."*

When someone believes the Truth and the lie at the same time, James says they are like a wave of the sea driven with the wind and tossed. He says that man is wavering, double-minded, and unstable in all of his ways. James says, "let not that man think that he shall receive anything of the Lord. A double minded man is unstable in *ALL* his ways."

The Word of God is a solid rock that gives you a sure foundation as you believe it and do it.

Believing the Truth and rejecting the lie is the simplest way of being delivered from fear. If the lie that is producing fear has been believed for so long that it has become a stronghold, then that could complicate the process, but deliverance is still possible once you know the Truth. The key to being delivered is, knowing and believing the Truth.

The Bible says God has given us weapons that are mighty through God for the pulling down of strong holds.

When the lying thought has become a stronghold, that can make it a lot more difficult to stop believing and thinking the lie.

A stronghold is an imagination, knowledge, or thought that has been fortified with impenetrable barriers, making it impossible to access in order to cause change.

A Stronghold is defined in the dictionary as: *a place that has been fortified so as to protect it against attack: a place where a particular cause or belief is strongly defended or upheld.*

This definition of a stronghold reveals why a strong hold of fear may be more difficult to overcome than the lie of fear.

With a stronghold, the lie is being defended by other lies or sometimes facts that make the lie seem true.

2 Corinthians 10:4-5 says, *"For though we walk in the flesh, we do not war after the flesh: (for the weapons of our warfare are not carnal, but mighty through God to the pulling down of strong holds;) casting down imaginations, and every high thing that exalteth itself against the knowledge of God, and bringing into captivity every thought to the obedience of Christ."*

Any imagination, knowledge, or thought that is contrary to the Word of God is a lie, and if you choose to believe that lie for an extended period of time, it could very easily become a stronghold.

Unfortunately, in too many cases, that's exactly what happens. The lie becomes a stronghold.

After it becomes a stronghold, it then takes the weapons of our warfare to take the thought captive, cast it down, and bring deliverance. The scripture says the weapons of our warfare are mighty through God to the pulling down of strongholds. The mightiness of our weapons comes through God by the Holy Spirit, not through our own cunning, strength or ability. Our weapons are mighty by the Anointing of the Holy Ghost.

Isaiah 10:27 says, *"And it shall come to pass in that day, that his burden shall be taken away from off thy shoulder, and his yoke from off thy neck, and the yoke shall be destroyed because of the anointing."*

The anointing removes the burden and destroys the yoke.

The anointing is the yoke-destroying, burden-removing power of the Holy Ghost.

Some of the weapons of our warfare are the Word of God,

the name of Jesus, the Blood of Jesus, and our Praise. All of these weapons are capable of pulling down any stronghold and setting the captive free.

John 8:32 says, *"and ye shall know the truth, and the truth shall make you free."*

The word "truth" in this verse is referring to the Word of God. The Word of God is Truth. It is anointed and capable of healing, delivering, and setting people free. The Word of God is the only Truth that exists in this world.

Philippians 2:9-10 says, *"Wherefore God also hath highly exalted him, and given him a name which is above every name: that at the name of Jesus every knee should bow, of things in heaven, and things in earth, and things under the earth."*

The name of Jesus is higher, the name of Jesus is greater, and the name of Jesus is stronger than anything that is named. The spirit of fear and everything that has a name has to bow in subjection to the name of the Lord Jesus Christ. There is no bondage or stronghold that can resist or withstand the name of Jesus.

The name of Jesus has the authority and power to heal the sick, cast out devils, set the captive free, and raise the dead. Pray using the name of Jesus and be set free from the spirit of fear.

Not long after I became a pastor, a gentleman brought a woman who was being tormented by a spirit of fear to church on a Friday night. This happened at a point in my ministry when I didn't have much experience in dealing with a spirit of fear, and I had never seen anyone tormented by a spirit of fear in this way or on this magnitude before. The woman was sobbing and had a look of sheer terror on her face the whole time that she was in church.

When I got the opportunity to minister to her, I found out that she was in fear because she had made a vow to the Lord and not kept it. Her fear was based on the Word of God where it speaks of the consequences of breaking a vow.

Ecclesiastes 5:4-6 says, *"When thou vowest a vow unto God, defer not to pay it; for he hath no pleasure in fools: pay that which thou hast vowed. Better is it that thou shouldest not vow, than that thou shouldest vow and not pay. Suffer not thy mouth to cause thy flesh to sin; neither say thou before the angel, that it was an error: wherefore should God be angry at thy voice, and destroy the work of thine hands?"*

Deuteronomy 23:21 says, *"When thou shalt vow a vow unto the LORD thy God, thou shalt not slack to pay it: for the LORD thy God will surely require it of thee; and it would be sin in thee."*

This poor woman believed that she was going to die and that God was going to destroy her family, because she had not kept her vow. So, I prayed the sinner's prayer with her and told her about the grace and mercy of God. I also told her that God was faithful and just to forgive us and cleanse us from all unrighteousness if we confess our sin. But no matter what I said, she wouldn't accept it. I saw where she was released for a brief moment but then went right back to believing the lie. That brief moment of release was when she rejected the lie, believed the Truth, and the Truth set her free. She was like Simon Peter who walked on water as long as he kept his eyes on Jesus, the Truth. The moment he took his eyes off of Jesus, he began to sink.

1 John 1:9 says, *"If we confess our sins, he is faithful and just to forgive us our sins, and to cleanse us from all unrighteousness."*

Matthew 14:29-30 says, *"And when Peter was come down*

out of the ship, he walked on the water, to go to Jesus. But when he saw the wind boisterous, he was afraid; and beginning to sink, he cried, saying, Lord, save me."

The other interesting thing about her fear is that it came as a result of her believing God's Word. It reminded me of when Jesus was tempted of the devil after being led by the Spirit into the wilderness for forty days. The devil said to Jesus, "it is written" and tried to use the scripture to get Jesus to worship him.

Luke 4:9-11 says, *"And he brought him to Jerusalem, and set him on a pinnacle of the temple, and said unto him, If thou be the Son of God, cast thyself down from hence: for it is written, He shall give his angels charge over thee, to keep thee: And in their hands they shall bear thee up, lest at any time thou dash thy foot against a stone."*

The devil was using the Word of God to make this woman believe his lie, just like he tried to do with Jesus.

The reason the devil's deception worked on this woman and it didn't work with Jesus is because Jesus knew the Word of God rightly divided. Jesus knew that the angels had been given charge over Him according to Psalm 91:11-12, but He also knew, "ye shalt not tempt the Lord your God" in Deuteronomy 6:16.

Her fear was created by the lie that God would not forgive her, and if God does not forgive her, then she would die, and her family would be destroyed.

It is amazing how much confusion, torment, and fear a lie can produce *when it is believed.*

When this woman came to church, this was the first time I had ever dealt with anything like this. At that time, I didn't know what I know today. So, unfortunately, she left church that night feeling a little better but still in bondage to the spirit of fear.

Since then, I have learned more about the Word of God, my authority and identity, and how fear works hand in hand with lies.

When I was in my early teens, my father told me about something that bothered him. He didn't say it caused fear, but I believe it did, because when I got older the same thing bothered me, and it made me fearful. I am thankful today that, by the grace of God, I no longer have that fear.

I find it interesting that my father's fear passed on to me simply by him telling me about it.

My father had a feeling, that feeling created a thought, and that thought produced fear. I only experienced that feeling and thought once or twice, but each time it produced fear. The feeling was real, but I realize today that the thought that the feeling produced was a lie.

I am also grateful that I didn't have the felling or thought long enough for it to become a stronghold.

My Dad also told me many, many things that produced faith. And today, as a result of those things that he told me, I am blessed to have a *Stronghold of Faith*. He told me about the miracles, signs, and wonders that he had seen and experienced. Those testimonies created thoughts, imaginations, and knowledge that then produced steadfast, unmovable, unshakeable, unwavering, immutable, determined, FAITH.

I wonder how many parents are passing their fears on to their children by either telling them about things that cause them fear, or by showing fear in certain situations. How many people have a fear of something, because they inherited it from a parent or relative?

Hebrews 2:14-15 says, *"Forasmuch then as the children are partakers of flesh and blood, he also himself likewise took part of the same; that through death he might destroy him that had the power of death, that is, the devil; and deliver them who through fear of death were all their lifetime subject to bondage."*

Jesus, through His death, overcame and destroyed the devil that had the power over death, and through His triumphant victory delivered us from the fear of death and its bondage.

Colossians 1:12-14 says, *"giving thanks unto the Father, which hath made us meet to be partakers of the inheritance of the saints in light: who hath delivered us from the power of darkness, and hath translated us into the kingdom of his dear Son: in whom we have redemption through his blood, even the forgiveness of sins."*

Fear is a spirit, and it is a part of the kingdom of darkness. Through the redemptive work of Jesus, we have been translated from the power and authority of darkness

into the Kingdom of God's dear Son, Jesus Christ. The devil and fear no longer have power over us unless we let them.

1 John 4:4 says, *"Ye are of God, little children, and have overcome them: because greater is he that is in you, than he that is in the world."*

The devil, demons, the spirit of fear, and the very gates of hell itself cannot prevail against you, because the Greater One is in you.

And because the Greater One, Jesus, is in you, that means all the fullness of the Godhead is dwelling in you *now*.

Colossians 2:9 says, *"For in him dwelleth all the fulness of the Godhead bodily."*

Matthew 16:18 says, *"And I say also unto thee, That thou art Peter, and upon this rock I will build my church; and the gates of hell shall not prevail against it."*

The gates of hell signify hell and everything associated with Satan and his kingdom not being able to prevail against you.

Romans 8:37 says, *"Nay, in all these things we are more than conquerors through him that loved us."*

You are more than a conqueror; you have the victory; God always causes you to triumph, and everything is and always will work together for your good. With all that going for you, the spirit of fear doesn't have a chance of remaining in your life unless you let it.

2 Corinthians 2:14 says, *"Now thanks be unto God, which always causeth us to triumph in Christ."*

Romans 8:28 says, *"And we know that all things work together for good to them that love God, to them who are the called according to his purpose."*

You have power over ALL the power of the enemy, and nothing the enemy does can hurt you. The *power* that Jesus said He gave us is translated from the Greek word *exusia*. *Exusia* means delegated authority. Jesus gave us His very own authority over all the power and abilities of the enemy. So, use your delegated authority. Open your mouth and cast out the spirit of fear in the name of Jesus. The spirit of fear does not have dominion over you—you have dominion over it. So tell fear to get lost!

Hit the road, fear, and don't you come back no more, no more, no more, no more.

Hebrews 2:14-15 says, *"Forasmuch then as the children are partakers of flesh and blood, he also himself likewise took part of the same; that through death he might destroy him that had the power of death, that is, the devil; and deliver them who through fear of death were all their lifetime subject to bondage."*

Again, we have been delivered from the bondage of the fear of death, because Jesus destroyed the devil that had the power of death. You are no longer a slave to fear. Fear does not have dominion over you. You're not a victim; you are a victor.

If you don't fear death, you won't have fear.

THE WAY OUT

The way out of a life of fear comes by knowing, believing, and acting on the Truth.

Deliverance from the spirit of fear starts with knowing the Truth.

In John 8:32, Jesus said, *"and ye shall know the truth, and the truth shall make you free."*

Knowing the Truth is just the starting point of being delivered from the spirit of fear. I say it is just the starting point, because a lot of people know the Truth but are yet held captive to the spirit of fear and many of the other tricks and traps of the devil.

A person can know the Truth and yet not believe it or act on it. A lot of people know about Jesus, His atoning and redemptive work, but continue to remain unrighteous and in bondage to fear because, even though they know about Jesus, they don't believe the Truth about who He is and what He has done.

It is only those who know and believe the Truth that are on the road to being made free from the spirit of fear.

Knowing and believing in who Jesus is and what He has done is the first step in being delivered from the spirit of fear.

1 John 4:18 says, *"There is no fear in love; but perfect love casteth out fear: because fear hath torment. He that feareth is not made perfect in **love**."*

Understanding who we are through the love of Christ Jesus causes love to be perfected and fear to be cast out. How can we fear when we know how much we are loved by God?

1 John 4:17 says, *"Herein is our love made perfect, that we may have boldness in the day of judgment: because as he is, so are we in this world."*

Our love is made perfect by knowing that, as He is, so are we in this world.

1 john 4:16 (TPT) says, *"By living in God, love has been brought to its full expression in us so that we may fearlessly face the day of judgment, because all that Jesus now is, so are we in this world."*

Through our living in God and God living in us, His love is brought to its full expression.

The next step in the process of being delivered from the spirit of fear is acting on the Truth.

Knowing the Truth is the first step, believing the Truth is step two, and acting on the Truth is step three. A person will never be completely free from the spirit of fear without knowing, believing, and acting on the Truth. These are the same three steps that are required in order to receive salvation.

You must not only know the Truth but must believe and act on it as well. Believe, confess, and do what God says.

The Word of God is not just true; it is TRUTH. In John 17:17, Jesus said the Word of God is truth: *"Sanctify them through thy truth: thy word is truth."*

Something can be true and yet not be Truth. In order for something to be considered Truth, it has to remain the same. It can't change, ever. Something can be true, but not Truth. True is temporary; it can and will change. Truth is eternal and will not change, ever. It is impossible for Truth to change.

Something can be true at 12:00 noon and not true at 12:01. But something that is Truth at 12:00 noon will be Truth at 12:01, 1:00, 2:30, and forever.

The only Truth that exists in this world is The Holy Bible, which is the Word of God. There are at least three places in the Bible where Jesus said, "Heaven and earth shall pass away, but my words shall not pass away" (Matthew 24:35, Mark 13:31, Luke 21:33). Truth is eternal and immutable.

Matthew 24:35 says, *"Heaven and earth shall pass away, but my words shall not pass away."*

People that are bound with the spirit of fear are bound because they have been deceived, and they have chosen to believe a lie rather than believe the Truth of God's Word. Anyone being tormented by fear because they are alone has that fear because they either don't know or they don't believe God's Word.

In Isaiah 43:1-5, God commands us not to fear:

"But now thus saith the LORD that created thee, O Jacob, and he that formed thee, O Israel, Fear not: for I have redeemed thee, I have called thee by thy name; thou art mine. When thou passest through the waters, I will be with thee; and through the rivers, they shall not overflow thee: when thou walkest through the fire, thou shalt not be burned; neither shall the flame kindle upon thee. For I am the LORD thy God, the Holy One of Israel, thy Saviour: I gave Egypt for thy ransom, Ethiopia and Seba for thee. Since thou wast precious in my sight, thou hast been honourable, and I have loved thee: therefore will I give men for thee, and people for thy life. Fear not: for I am with thee."

The first thing God says in Isaiah 43:1 is, *"Fear not: for I have redeemed thee."*

God says we have no reason to fear, because He has redeemed us. Redeemed us means: *he ransomed us, to compensate for the faults or bad aspects of (something). Gain or regain possession of (something) in exchange for payment.* So, this means we belong to God, we are His property, and God knows how to take care of what belongs to Him.

The second thing God says is: *Fear not: for I am with the!* So believe by faith that God is with you. Stop believing the lie that you are all by yourself, you're all alone, and it's you against the world.

Hebrews 11:27 says, *"By faith he forsook Egypt, not fearing the wrath of the king: for he endured, as seeing him who is invisible."*

By faith Moses forsook Egypt. He didn't fear the wrath of the king, because he was behaving as though he could see God right there with him. My Dad used to call that, *practicing the presence of God.*

Practicing the presence of God is when you accept by faith that God is with you, acknowledge His presence, and then behave like God is right there with you, because He is.

You cannot practice the presence of God and be in fear at the same time. The moment you acknowledge God's presence, fear can't stay. So you should be constantly reminding yourself that God is with you, and as you do, the spirit of fear will flee. Be like Moses and behave as though you see God right there with you all the time.

Hebrews 13:5-6 says, *"Let your conversation be without covetousness; and be content with such things as ye have: for he hath said, I will never leave thee, nor forsake thee. So that we may boldly say, The Lord is my helper, and I will not fear What man shall do unto me."*

What can the devil or anyone do to you if God is with you?

In Isaiah 54:17, God said, *"No weapon that is formed against thee shall prosper; and every tongue that shall rise against thee in judgment thou shalt condemn."*

Make your way out of fear by believing, the weapon your enemy has formed against you will not prosper; it won't work. Believe that you will condemn every judgmental, wicked, negative word that is spoken against you. Believe the Truth. Believe what God says. Know the Truth, believe the Truth, and act on it by faith.

Jesus Christ purchased our salvation two thousand years ago. It is available to anyone who will receive it by faith. Salvation is more than just the forgiveness of your sins, the gift of the Holy Spirit, and eternal life. Salvation is also deliverance from the spirit of fear, sickness, disease, poverty, all the works of the devil, and everything negative that came into the world through the sin of Adam.

Colossians 1:12-13 says, *"giving thanks unto the Father, which hath made us meet to be partakers of the inheritance of the saints in light: who hath delivered us from the power of darkness, and hath translated us into the kingdom of his dear Son: in whom we have redemption through his blood, even the forgiveness of sins."*

We have been delivered from all the powers of darkness and translated in the Kingdom of God's dear Son, Jesus Christ. That means the spirit of fear no longer has dominion over us unless we allow it.

Joshua 24:15 says, *"choose you this day whom ye will serve."*

It says choose, because you have a choice, and that's ultimately what it all comes down to: your choice.

So are you going to continue to serve sin and live in bondage to the spirit of fear, or will you choose to reject sin and its lies and live a life of freedom and peace?

I strongly suggest that you choose to reject the lie, believe the Truth, enter into God's rest, and receive His peace.

You come out of fear just like you come out of anything else, one step at a time. The first step is believing in the Lord Jesus Christ and receiving Him as Savior and Lord. This first step delivers you from the powers of darkness and translates you into the Kingdom of Jesus, the Son of God. One of the next steps is finding a good church where you can be taught the Word of God.

Hosea 4:6 says, *"My people are destroyed for lack of knowledge: because thou hast rejected knowledge, I will also reject thee, that thou shalt be no priest to me."*

It is extremely important to know the Truth, because knowing the Truth will not only make you free, but it will also keep you free.

When tribulation (trouble) comes—and it will because Jesus said it would—don't believe the lie that says, "This is going to ruin you" or "You're going to lose everything." No! Those thoughts are a lie. They are from your adversary the devil. Believe the Truth. Be of good cheer and believe what God says.

Believe that your Heavenly Father is going to turn it all around and make it all work together for your good.

John 16:33 says, *"These things I have spoken unto you, that in me ye might have peace. In the world ye shall have tribulation: but be of good cheer; I have overcome the world."*

Jesus has overcome the world and all of its tribulations,

so cheer up. He has done everything necessary to see to it that you triumph and succeed.

Romans 8:28 says, *"And we know that all things work together for good to them that love God, to them who are the called according to his purpose."*

God has promised to make everything work together for your good. So trust that God will do what He said and stop the fear.

Believe what God said in 2 Corinthians 2:14: *"Now thanks be unto God, which <u>always</u> causeth us to triumph in Christ."*

Believe 1 Corinthians 15:57 that says, *"But thanks be to God, which giveth us the victory through our Lord Jesus Christ."*

God says He gives us the victory and He always causes us to triumph. If you believe what God says, then you will not fear.

Numbers 23:19 says, *"God is not a man, that he should lie; Neither the son of man, that he should repent: Hath he said, and shall he not do it?"*

Titus 1:2 says, *"in hope of eternal life, which God, that cannot <u>lie</u>, promised before the world began."*

Hebrews 6:18 says, *"that by two immutable things, in which it was impossible for God to lie, we might have a strong consolation, who have fled for refuge to lay hold upon the hope set before us."*

Isaiah 55:11 says, *"so shall my word be that goeth forth out of my mouth: it shall not return unto me void, but it shall accomplish that which I please, and it shall prosper in the thing whereto I sent it."*

God is not a man that He should lie; God cannot lie; it is impossible for God to lie, and God's Word will always accomplish their assignment and prosper in the thing He sent it to do.

I believe God. *He Cannot Lie!* Therefore, I will not fear!

Stop believing the lie and start believing the Truth.

REFUSE TO FEAR!

Say this: *I REFUSE TO FEAR!*

If you're thinking, "That sounds so simple," that's because that's exactly what it is: simple!

Jesus has already done the hard part for you.

FEAR OR FAITH

In Hebrews 11:6, it says, *"But without faith it is impossible to please him: for he that cometh to God must believe that he is, and that he is a rewarder of them that diligently seek him."*

That verse makes us aware of how important faith is in our relationship with God.

Faith is so important that it is impossible to please God without faith.

We established in a previous chapter that fear is faith's evil twin. So based on that we could also say, without fear it is impossible to please the devil.

The devil needs fear just like God needs faith. Satan is the rewarder of those that diligently fear him.

If you're walking in faith, you can't have fear, and if you're walking in fear, you can't have faith. Fear and faith have the same function, but they are a part of two different kingdoms. There is no fear in the Kingdom of God, and there is no faith in the kingdom of darkness. If you are in the Kingdom of God, then you have to walk by faith and not by sight.

2 Corinthians 5:7 says, *"for we walk by faith, not by sight."*

If you are in the kingdom of darkness, then you have to walk by sight, feelings, reality, and facts. This is what allows fear to work.

Mark 9:23 says, *"Jesus said unto him, If thou canst believe, all things are possible to him that believeth."*

When Jesus said *all things* are possible, that is exactly what He meant. *It is your believing that makes the impossible*

possible! Jesus said this to a man whose son was demon possessed. In the natural, his request for help was impossible, but in the spirit, if he could just believe, his believing would make the impossible possible.

Your believing something is what makes it possible, whether it be good or bad, positive or negative. It is your believing that turns it from impossible to possible.

Your believing authorizes, empowers, and makes it take place.

Fear and Faith function exactly alike and have the same purpose. Fear is faith's shadow. Fear and faith are what allow the devil or God to operate in your life. Fear authorizes the devil, while faith authorizes God.

Faith allows God to fulfill His plan and purpose in your life. Faith pleases God. Faith allows you to access and activate the power and presence of God in your life.

Hebrews 11:1 says, *"Now faith is the substance of things hoped for, the evidence of things not seen."*

The same could be said about fear. *"Now fear is the substance of things hoped for, the evidence of things not seen."*

I have an old Living Translation of Hebrews 11:1 that says it this way. *"What is faith? It is the confident assurance that something we want is going to happen. It is the certainty that what we hope for is waiting for us, even though we cannot see it up ahead."*

Faith is the confident assurance and certainty that what God has said is going to happen.

Fear is the confident assurance and certainty that what the devil has said is going to happen.

The purpose of Fear is the same as faith, but it gives the devil access and authority to fulfill his plan and purpose in your life. Fear pleases the devil just like faith pleases God. Fear authorizes the devil to access and activate his power and presence of in your life.

Job said, *"For the thing which I greatly feared is come upon me, And that which I was afraid of is come unto me"* (Job 3:25).

Job's fear broke the hedge of protection that was around him, which then gave Satan access to destroy all that he had.

Job 1:10 says, *"Hast not thou made an hedge about him, and about his house, and about all that he hath on every side?"*

Hebrews 11:1 in the Classic Amplified Version of the Bible says, *"NOW FAITH is the assurance (the confirmation, the title deed) of the things [we] hope for, being the proof of things [we] do not see and the conviction of their reality [faith perceiving as real fact what is not revealed to the senses]."*

Let's superimpose the word fear into that verse.

"NOW FEAR is the assurance (the confirmation, the title deed) of the things [we] hope for, being the proof of things [we] do not see and the conviction of their reality [fear perceiving as real fact what is not revealed to the senses]."

It's the same Biblical reference only about two different things.

Just as God was able to accomplish all of the miraculous things in Hebrews 11 through faith in His Word, Satan is also able to accomplish his works through fear of his lies.

Your faith, just like your fear, is the confident assurance and certainty that it will happen. That is why it can and why it does, whether it is of God or of the devil.

Just as God needs faith to accomplish His Will in your life, Satan needs fear to accomplish and do his will in your life. So, fear and faith have the same function. They are the currency through which God and Satan accomplish their will and manifest their works.

Fear is faith's evil cousin! It is faith's shadow.

Just as faith comes by hearing, fear comes by hearing as well.

Romans 10:17 says, *"So then faith cometh by hearing, and hearing by the word of God."*

In order for fear to work, you have to walk by sight, facts, and reality.

James 2:17 says, *"Even so faith, if it hath not works, is dead, being alone."*

James 2:26 says, *"For as the body without the spirit is dead, so faith without works is dead also."*

Faith without works is dead. Works is corresponding action or corresponding deeds.

Fear must also be accompanied with works or deeds. So, I could also say, fear without works is dead, being alone.

When you really have faith in something, that faith will move you to act.

When you believe something to the point of acting on it, then you're in faith. If you believe a lie to the point of acting on it, you're in fear. Fear will make you run when no one is chasing you, all because you believe you're being chased.

Mark 11:23 says, *"For verily I say unto you, That whosoever shall say unto this mountain, Be thou removed, and be thou cast into the sea; and shall not doubt in his heart, but shall believe that those things which he saith shall come to pass; he shall have whatsoever he saith."*

The same can be said of fear. If you have fear and doubt not, you will also have what you say.

Through fear just like through faith, you speak to things, and they obey you.

Mark 11:24 says, *"Therefore I say unto you, What things soever ye desire, when ye pray, believe that ye receive them, and ye shall have them."*

This also applies with fear. Anything that you believe you receive, you will have. Through fear, if you believe you receive it, you will have it.

Hebrews 11:3 *"Through faith we understand that the worlds were framed by the word of God, so that things which are seen were not made of things which do appear."*

You frame your world with words spoken in faith or fear. Everything spoken about faith can be said about fear as well.

Fear is a spirit. Being afraid, frightened, and scared are emotions, but fear is a spirit. Fear comes when there is nothing to be afraid or fearful of. Fear lies and tells you that you should be afraid. Fear's purpose is to get you to allow the devil to dominate and control your life.

FEAR CANNOT BE ALLOWED OR TOLERATED IN ANY AREA OF YOUR LIFE.

Faith is also called a spirit in 2 Corinthians 4:13.

"We having the same spirit of faith, according as it is written, I believed, and therefore have I spoken; we also believe, and therefore speak."

God does not use fear to motivate us or to confirm His

Word. God confirms His Word with the fruit of the Spirit, and He motivates us with His Love and blessings.

1 John 4:18 says, *"There is no fear in love; but perfect love casteth out fear: because fear hath torment. He that feareth is not made perfect in love."*

God is love! So, if there is no fear in love, then there is no fear in God.

This verse also says "perfect love *casteth out fear.*" The reason the term "casteth" out is used is, because fear is a spirit and it has to be cast out.

2 Timothy 1:7 says, *"For God hath not given us the spirit of fear; but of power, and of love, and of a sound mind."*

Paul calls fear a spirit, and because it is a spirit, it has to be cast out. Emotions and feelings can be changed, but fear has to be cast out.

ALL FEAR is a product of the fear of death, and if allowed, it will produce bondage and torment.

Hebrews 2:15 says, *"And deliver them who through fear of death were all their lifetime subject to bondage."*

If you heard a loud noise that startled you, you might be frightened and feel afraid. You can't stop those feelings from happening, but you can control them if they do.

Unexpected things can frighten you temporally, but you should never stay frightened or afraid.

Part of being frightened comes from the unknown. Not knowing what caused the noise can cause you to be afraid or frightened, but once the source of the noise is known, then the feeling of being afraid should leave. If you still feel afraid even after the source of the noise is known, then you're no longer dealing with emotions, you're dealing with a spirit of fear.

Something can start with your emotions and then become spiritual.

Emotions are triggered by something that you experience with your five senses. Fear, on the other hand, can come with no reason or explanation at all. Fear is a spirit. Fear has no rhyme or reason.

Always choose faith over fear, because you have a choice, and you can. If you choose to reject faith and allow fear, you will live in torment, because fear hath torment.

1 John 4:18 says, *"There is no fear in love; but perfect love casteth out fear: because fear hath torment. He that feareth is not made perfect in love."*

People who fear live in torment. They are constantly being bombarded with the thought that something bad is going to happen or that they're going to die. They live in fear of something happening to them or someone they care about. That's torment.

So choose faith, resist fear, and fear will flee from you.

James 4:7 says, *"Submit yourselves therefore to God. Resist the devil, and he will flee from you."*

Choosing to have faith and believe God is resisting the devil.

WORRY IS FEAR

Worry is fear. Worry is an indication that you are in fear of something. You might be worrying about something in the past, the present, or the future, but make no mistake about it; your worrying is fear.

Again, the dictionary definition of fear is: *a distressing emotion aroused by impending danger, evil, pain, etc., whether the threat is real or imagined; the* feeling or condition of being afraid.

Worry is thinking something dangerous, evil, or painful is going to happen, whether the possibility of it happening is real or imagined.

In Matthew 6:25, Jesus said, *"Therefore I say unto you, Take no thought for your life, what you shall eat, or what you shall drink; nor yet for your body, what you shall put on. Is not the life more than meat, and the body than raiment?"*

The literal translation of "Take no thought" is: Do not worry, or don't be anxious.

I believe the reason Jesus said take no thought instead of just saying do not worry is because a lot of people don't know what worry actually is, and so they don't realize that they worry.

So, Jesus used the phrase take no thought, because it actually describes what worry is. Worry, is taking or using thoughts to think about the what, the where, the when, and the how of life. Worry is fear, and like all fears, it has its origin in the fear of death. Worry is also based on a lie.

Jesus said not to worry about <u>what</u> you will eat, <u>what</u> you will drink, or <u>what</u> you will wear. Food, drink, and clothing are the basic necessities of life. Without them you will die, and the fear of death is the root of all worry and fear.

It is the fear of death that causes you to worry or think about these things and that opens the door to the spirit of fear. The lie that creates worry or fear is: You won't have any or enough of the basic necessities to live.

Proverbs 3:25 says, *"Be not afraid of sudden fear, Neither of the desolation of the wicked, when it cometh."*

Some translations translate this verse as sudden disaster or sudden terror. I believe God is telling us not to worry about disaster, trouble, terror, or any unknown problems that could seemingly come up out of nowhere. A lot of people are worried about things that will never happen and, in most cases, never do. Don't worry and be in fear about what might happen. Instead, have faith that God will do what He said He would do.

Have faith in what you know will happen instead of worrying about what you believe might happen.

A few days ago, while in the process of writing this book, the Lord asked me a question. He asked, "Why are you worried?" I didn't think I was worried about anything, so I immediately assumed that He asked this question so that I could minister to my church and others about worry. The reality was, the question was not only for my church but also for me, because unbeknownst to me I had been worrying about something that I was going through without realizing it. I thank God for His love, mercy, and grace!

I hope you realize that, whenever God asks a question, it is never because there is something He doesn't know. God asks questions because there is something that He wants you to know. He asks questions because you have freewill, and He can't tell you things without your permission.

So God asked me "Why are you worried?" for two reasons. One is because He wanted me to know that I was worrying, and secondly, He wanted me to know that I had no reason to worry.

God told me the reason I was worrying was, *"Because you don't trust the covenant."*

God is a God of covenant. He is a covenant-making and covenant-keeping God. The word covenant means: agreement, contract, or promise.

The Bible is the Word of God, and it is His Covenant. Those of us who believe and trust His Covenant (the Word of God) will not worry. Worry comes when we don't believe, trust, or remember God's Covenant to help us, provide for us, protect us, and so much more. The Children of Israel spent forty years in the wilderness, because they didn't believe, trust, or remember God's covenant and all that He had done for them.

Instead, they worried and murmured about they're food, water, and every difficulty along the way.

Worry is a sign that you believe something is possible. So, if you're worrying, it is because you believe the thing you're thinking about could happen.

Mark 9:23 says, *"Jesus said unto him, If thou canst believe, all things are possible to him that believeth."*

When Jesus said *all things* are possible, that is exactly what He meant. All things include good things, bad things, evil things, and wicked things. All things mean all things, even if the thing is impossible.

The impossible becomes possible when you believe it can happen.

Your believing is the faith that makes the impossible possible. Your believing authorizes, empowers, and causes it to take happen. Worry is fear and fear is faith's evil counterpart. Faith and fear have the ability to produce the impossible. Fear functions just like faith.

Hebrews 11:1 says, *"Now faith is the substance of things hoped for, the evidence of things not seen."*

Fear, like faith, is the substance of things hoped for, the evidence of things not seen. And just as God was able to accomplish all of the miracles in Hebrews 11 through faith in Him and His Word, Satan is able to accomplish his works through fear of him and his word. Your faith, just like your fear, is the confident assurance and certainty that it will happen. Whether it is of God or of the devil.

Just as God needs faith to accomplish His Will in your life, Satan needs fear to accomplish and do his will in your life. So, fear and faith have the same function.

They are the vehicles through which God and Satan accomplish their will and manifest their work in our lives. Fear is faith's evil twin! It is faith's shadow. Fear also comes like faith, by hearing.

Romans 10:17 says, *"So then faith cometh by hearing, and hearing by the word of God."*

In like manner, fear comes by hearing, and hearing by the lies spoken by the devil.

2 Corinthians 5:7 says, *"for we walk by faith, not by sight."*

In order for fear to work, you have to walk by sight and not by faith. Walking by sight is, walking by your five senses, facts, and reality. It is living and making decisions based on what you see, hear, feel, taste and touch.

The spirit of fear needs all of these things to succeed.

Fear or faith: The choice is yours. You have to decide whether you're going to walk in faith or walk in fear.

If we substituted the word fear in Mark 11:23, it would look like this. *For verily I say unto you, That whosoever shall say unto this mountain, Be thou removed, and be thou cast into the sea; and shall not doubt in his heart, but shall fear that those things which he saith shall come to pass; he shall have whatsoever he saith.*

If you have fear and don't doubt, you will have what you say.

Through fear, if you believe you receive it, you will have it.

Through fear, you speak to things, and they obey you.

Hebrews 11:3 *"Through faith we understand that the worlds were framed by the word of God, so that things which are seen were not made of things which do appear."*

What if we changed Hebrews 11:3 like we did with Mark 11:23?

Through *fear,* we understand that your world was framed by the lie of Satan, so that things which are seen were not made of things which do appear. You frame your world through words spoken in fear or faith.

Fear is a spirit. Being afraid, frightened, or scared are emotions. Fear comes when there is nothing to be afraid or fearful of. Fear lies and tells you that you should be afraid. Fear wants to dominate and control your life. Fear cannot be allowed or tolerated in any area of your life.

God will never use fear to confirm His Word. One of the ways that God confirms His Word is with the fruit of the Spirit. God could tell you the worst thing you can think of is going to happen, and yet you will have a peace about it that you cannot explain. That peace is God confirming His Word.

God confirms His Word with the fruit of the Spirit: love, joy, peace, and so on. If you ever get a word and it produces fear, that fear is the sign that that word was not from God.

Fear will never produce love, joy, peace, or any of the fruit of the Spirit. The only thing that fear produces is torment and more fear. Faith will always yield a manifestation of the fruit of the Spirit and more faith.

Romans 1:17 says, *"For therein is the righteousness of God revealed from faith to faith: as it is written, The just shall live by faith."*

2 Timothy 1:7 says, *"For God hath not given us the spirit of fear; but of power, and of love, and of a sound mind."*

Paul calls fear a spirit, and because fear is a spirit, it has to be cast out. Emotions can be changed, but fear has to be cast out.

If you hear a loud noise that startles you, you might be frightened and feel afraid. You can't stop those feelings from coming, but you can control them if they do.

Part of being frightened comes from the unknown. Not knowing what caused the noise can stir up your emotions and cause you to be afraid, but once the source of the noise is known, then the feeling of being afraid should leave.

If you still feel afraid even after the source of the noise is known, then you are no longer dealing with emotions; you're dealing with a spirit of fear.

Something can start out through your emotions and then evolve into something spiritual.

Emotions are triggered by something that you experience

with your five senses. Fear, on the other hand, comes with no reason or explanation at all. Fear is a spirit.

THE FEAR OF THE UNKNOWN

I believe the fear of the unknown has a name: It's called WORRY.

Worry is having a fear of the unknown. The unknown could be things you can't explain, things you don't know, or things you are unaware of. In most cases, worry is a fear of things in the future.

The dictionary definition of worry is: *a state of anxiety and uncertainty over actual or potential problems.* Fear of actual problems happens as a result of not knowing how those problems will turn out. Whereas, fear of potential problems happen because of the possibility of something becoming a problem.

If you are born again and in covenant with God, then you never have to fear the unknown, because God is omniscient. He is all knowing. God knows the past, the present, and the future. He knows what will happen before it happens, and He has promised to give you the victory, always causes you to triumph, and makes it all work together for your good.

In Matthew 6:8, Jesus said, *"Be not ye therefore like unto them: for your Father knoweth what things ye have need of, before ye ask him."*

God knows what you need before you ask for it. He even knows your thoughts before you think them.

Matt. 9:4 says, *"And Jesus knowing their thoughts said, Wherefore think ye evil in your hearts?"*

Psalms 139:4 says, *"Thou knowest my downsitting and*

mine uprising, thou understandest my thought afar off."

So, in Matthew 6:25 Jesus said, *"Therefore I say unto you, Take no thought for your life, what ye shall eat, or what ye shall drink; nor yet for your body, what ye shall put on. Is not the life more than meat, and the body than raiment?"*

The term "take no thought" is translated: *stop being worried or anxious about your life*, in the Amplified Version of the Bible. In the King James Version it literally means: Do not worry.

When Jesus said, "take no thought," He was literally describing what worry is. I believe He said it that way because most people don't really know what worrying is.

All of the things in Matthew 6:25-33 that Jesus told us not to worry about are all a part of the unknown future.

The number one reason why believers do not have to fear the unknown is, *COVENANT!* God is a covenant-making and covenant-keeping God. His covenants cover everything that could potentially happen to us in this life, from now until Jesus returns.

In Psalm 89:34, God says, *"My covenant will I not break, nor alter the thing that is gone out of my lips."*

Psalm 23:1 says, *"The LORD is my shepherd; I shall not want."*

The Lord says He is your shepherd, which makes Him responsible for everything you want, need, or desire. So you should never fear that you won't have something that you want, need, or desire.

Psalm 34:4 says, *"I sought the LORD, and he heard me, And delivered me from all my fears."*

God can and God will deliver you from all of your fears, even the fear of the unknown, if you let Him.

One of the ways God delivers us from the fear of the unknown is by reminding us that He is always with us.

Isaiah 43:1-5 says, *"But now thus saith the LORD that created thee, O Jacob, and he that formed thee, O Israel, Fear not: for I have redeemed thee, I have called thee by thy name; thou art mine. When thou passest through the waters, I will be with thee; and through the rivers, they shall not overflow thee: when thou walkest through the fire, thou shalt not be burned; neither shall the flame kindle upon thee. For I am the LORD thy God, the Holy One of Israel, thy Saviour: I gave Egypt for thy ransom, Ethiopia and Seba for thee. Since thou wast precious in my sight, thou hast been honourable, and I have loved thee: therefore will I give men for thee, and people for thy life. Fear not: for I am with thee."*

Matthew 28:18-20 says, *"And Jesus came and spake unto them, saying, All power is given unto me in heaven and in earth. Go ye therefore, and teach all nations, baptizing them in the name of the Father, and of the Son, and of the Holy Ghost: teaching them to observe all things whatsoever I have commanded you: and, lo, I am with you alway, even unto the end of the world. Amen."*

Jesus is always with me. Therefore, *I WILL NOT FEAR!*

Hebrews 13:5-6 says, *"Let your conversation be without covetousness; and be content with such things as ye have: for he hath said, I will never leave thee, nor forsake thee. So that we may boldly say, The Lord is my helper, and I will not fear What man shall do unto me."*

The Lord will never leave me or forsake me. He is my helper. I will not fear what mere men may do to me.

Isaiah 45:2 says, *"I will go before thee, and make the crooked places straight: I will break in pieces the gates of brass, and cut in sunder the bars of iron."*

God said He will go ahead of us and make the crooked places straight. That means everywhere we go, God has already been there, straightening out and fixing all of the crooked things before we arrive.

Isaiah 54:17 says, *"No weapon that is formed against thee shall prosper; and every tongue that shall rise against thee in judgment thou shalt condemn. This is the heritage of the servants of the LORD, and their righteousness is of me, saith the LORD."*

The Bible tells us that we have an adversary, the devil. It doesn't tell us the exact plans and weapons that he is forming against us, but it does tell us that whatever weapons he is forming, they will not prosper; they will not work.

These are just a couple of the covenant promises that God has made with us. They are examples of why we don't ever have to fear the unknown.

Proverbs 3:5-6 says, *"Trust in the LORD with all thine heart; And lean not unto thine own understanding. In all thy ways acknowledge him, And he shall direct thy paths."*

If you follow these instructions and acknowledge the Lord in all of your ways, then He will direct you and show you which paths to take. You won't ever have to worry about where you're going or how it will turn out, because the Lord is directing it all.

John 16:13 says, *"Howbeit when he, the Spirit of truth, is come, he will guide you into all truth: for he shall not speak of himself; but whatsoever he shall hear, that shall he speak: and he will shew you things to come."*

Jesus said, when the Spirit of Truth is come, He will guide you into all truth, and He will show you things to come. The Holy Spirit guides us and shows us things to come. That means we will know about Spiritual and natural things before they happen. I think that makes us more than conquerors and always causes us to triumph.

Romans 8:28 says, *"And we know that all things work together for good to them that love God, to them who are the called according to his purpose."*

God has promised to make all things work together for your good. All things include the known and the unknown.

1 Corinthians 2:6-8 says, *"Howbeit we speak wisdom among them that are perfect: yet not the wisdom of this world, nor of the princes of this world, that come to nought: but we speak the wisdom of God in a mystery, even the hidden wisdom, which God ordained before the world unto our glory: which none of the princes of this world knew: for had they known it, they would not have crucified the Lord of glory."*

God knew that Adam would sin, so He prepared a plan of redemption before he actually needed it. God also knows everything that will happen in your life and has in the same way prepared a plan for your sins, faults, and failures as well.

Revelations 13:8 says, *"And all that dwell upon the earth shall worship him, whose names are not written in the book of life of the Lamb slain from the foundation of the world."*

Jesus is called the lamb slain from the foundation of the world. This is confirmation that nothing surprises God—not Adams sin, our sin, or anything that the devil may attempt to do.

Matthew 2:12-13 says, *"And being warned of God in a dream that they should not return to Herod, they departed into their own country another way. And when they were departed, behold, the angel of the Lord appeareth to Joseph in a dream, saying, Arise, and take the young child and his mother, and flee into Egypt, and be thou there until I bring thee word: for Herod will seek the young child to destroy him."*

The Wise Men and Joseph were warned of Herod's plans in a dream. God will do the same thing for us. In John 16:13, Jesus said the Holy Spirit would guide us and show us things to come.

Colossians 3:2-3 says, *"Set your affection on things above, not on things on the earth. For ye are dead, and your life is hid with Christ in God."*

We shouldn't be focused on the things of this world. Our focus should be on the things of God and His Word. Our old life is dead and gone. We are born again, new creatures in Christ Jesus, and our new life is hidden with Christ in God. Hidden means the devil doesn't know God's plan for our life, nor does he have access to it or the ability to change it.

These are just a few of the reason that we should not fear the unknown. Many things may be unknown to us, but our Heavenly Father knows it all.

So, instead of worrying and being anxious, pray.

Ephesians 4:6-8 says, *"Be careful for nothing; but in every thing by prayer and supplication with thanksgiving let your requests be made known unto God. And the peace of God, which passeth all understanding, shall keep your hearts and minds through Christ Jesus. Finally, brethren, whatsoever things are true, whatsoever things are honest, whatsoever things are just, whatsoever things are pure, whatsoever things are lovely, whatsoever things are of good report; if there be any virtue, and if there be any praise, think on these things."*

If you follow the instructions in Ephesians 4:6-8, you will walk in peace that passes all understanding, peace that cannot be understood or explained.

1 Samuel 17:32-37 says, *"And David said to Saul, Let no man's heart fail because of him; thy servant will go and fight with this Philistine. And Saul said to David, Thou art not able to go against this Philistine to fight with him: for thou art but a youth, and he a man of war from his youth. And David said unto Saul, Thy servant kept his father's sheep, and there came a lion, and a bear, and took a lamb out of the flock: and I went out after him, and smote him, and delivered it out of his mouth: and when he arose against me, I caught him by his beard, and smote him, and slew him. Thy servant slew both the lion and the bear: and this uncircumcised Philistine shall be as one of them, seeing he hath defied the armies of the living God. David said moreover, The LORD that delivered me out of the paw of the lion, and out of the paw of the bear, he will deliver me out of the hand of this Philistine. And Saul said unto David, Go, and the LORD be with thee."*

When the lion and bear came into the camp, David had no idea that it was preparation for what was coming. God used the lion and bear to prepare David to fight Goliath.

We don't know when a Goliath will show up in our life, but we can rest assured that God knows, and He will see to it that we are prepared to meet and defeat him when he does.

We have no reason to fear the unknown, because nothing is unknown to our God.

FEAR COMETH BY HEARING

The Bible says in Romans 10:17, *"So then faith cometh by hearing, and hearing by the word of God."*

I believe fear comes in the same way, by hearing.

In March of 2019, the President of the United States and other world leaders declared that we were in a pandemic, because of the Novel Coronavirus or Covid-19. Although most people probably didn't know exactly what that meant, it immediately created a sense of fear and uncertainty. That fear and uncertainty was then fueled by frequent government news conferences and the news media, who constantly bombarded us with reports of how many people had died, how many people were in the ICU, and how many positive cases and hospitalizations there were from this deadly virus. Fear came by hearing.

The fear that people experienced and, in some cases, still experience was all born out of hearing the reports of a new virus and the devastating effects that it was having on billions of people all over the world.

In the case of Covid-19, it wasn't that everything we were being told was a lie. It was the unknown aspects and effects of the virus that produced fear. Not knowing exactly how it was contracted or how it would affect you if you contracted it created anxiety and fear.

Although the majority of people around the world did not contract the virus or die from it, many people were and still are living in fear of the possibility today.

During the pandemic, if you were in a remote part of the world that didn't have Internet access or news media coverage, you probably would have been living your life with peace of mind, totally unaware and unaffected by what was happening in countries around the world, because you never heard about it. Fear, like faith, comes by hearing.

James 2:26 says, *"For as the body without the spirit is dead, so faith without works is dead also."*

Just as faith without works is dead, so also fear without works is dead. The word "works" in verse 26 can also be translated *corresponding action*. So fear, just like faith, has to be accompanied by works or corresponding action; otherwise it is dead. Calling it dead means it cannot do or accomplish anything.

Anything you hear that is contrary to the Word of God is a lie. Do not allow bad news, a negative report, or a bad diagnosis to produce fear. All of these things are facts, which means they are subject to change. Facts are true, but they are not Truth. Truth can't change. The Word of God is the only Truth that exists in this world. It is impossible for the Word of God to change. We change facts by simply believing and confessing the Truth over them.

GOD AND THE DEVIL WANT AND NEED THE SAME THING

As strange and as outrageous this title may sound, it is true. God and the devil want and need the same thing, and they need it for the same reason.

They both need you to believe.

God and the devil need you to believe. God cannot work in your life without you having faith in Him and in His Word. In the same way, the devil cannot work in your life without you having fear of him and his lies.

In Genesis 2:16-17, God said, *"And the LORD God commanded the man, saying, Of every tree of the garden thou mayest freely eat: but of the tree of the knowledge of good and evil, thou shalt not eat of it: for in the day that thou eatest thereof thou shalt surely die."*

In Genesis 3:4-5, Satan said, *"And the serpent said unto the woman, Ye shall not surely die: for God doth know that in the day ye eat thereof, then your eyes shall be opened, and ye shall be as gods, knowing good and evil."*

God told them eating the fruit of the tree of the knowledge of good and evil would bring death. Satan told the woman they wouldn't die, but rather, eating the fruit would make them as gods, knowing good and evil. Their life and how they would live all came down to who they believed, just like it is for us today. If we believe God and His Word, we will have life and that more abundantly. If we choose to believe the devil and his lie, then we will live separated from God in torment under the fear of death.

PERFECT LOVE CASTS OUT FEAR

1 John 4:18 says, *"Perfect love casteth out fear."*

It says, "casteth out" because fear is a spirit, and it must be cast out. Some translations say perfect love drives out fear, banishes fear, or expels fear. Either way, fear must be compelled to leave. There are several ways to cast out a spirit of fear. Some of these ways have been discussed in other chapters.

When you confront fear as a spirit and you understand the authority that you have in Christ Jesus as a born again, Spirit-filled child of God, you will be victorious over fear every time.

Perfect love cast out fear simply means that, when you fully understand how much your sovereign God loves you, that revelation will cast out all fear.

John 3:16 says, *"For God so loved the world, that he gave his only begotten Son, that whosoever believeth in him should not perish, but have everlasting life."*

Perfect Love is what moved God to give His only begotten Son as a sacrifice for our sin. Fear cannot abide where a revelation of God's perfect love exists.

1 John 3:16 says, *"Hereby perceive we the love of God, because he laid down his life for us: and we ought to lay down our lives for the brethren."*

We perceive the magnitude of God's love through the sacrifice that He made for us. He loved us so much that He died for us. And when you understand how much God loves you, you don't fear His judgment.

John 5:13 says, *"Greater love hath no man than this, that a man lay down his life for his friends."*

Fear is a spirit of deception that is manifested through believing a lie.

NOTES

CONTACT INFORMATION

Please send your prayer request, comments, questions, and book orders to us at:

Deliverance Revival Tabernacle PO Box 3642

Plymouth, MA 02361

You can also visit the website at: EIOSBORNE.ORG

Deliverance Revival Tabernacle

Copyright© 2024

Printed in the USA
CPSIA information can be obtained
at www.ICGtesting.com
JSHW012132290824
68836JS00005B/13